COPYCATS

42 CREATIVE ARTISAN PROJECTS TO MAKE

& ARTIFACTS

MARIANNE FORD

drawings by ANNA PUGH

DAVID R. GODINE · PUBLISHER · BOSTON

First U.S. edition published in 1986 by
David R. Godine, Publisher, Inc.
Horticultural Hall
300 Massachusetts Avenue
Boston, Massachusetts 02115

First published in 1983 in the U.K. by André Deutsch Ltd.

Library of Congress Cataloging-in-Publication Data

Ford, Marianne.
    Copycats and artifacts.

    Originally published as: Copycats. 1983.
    Bibliography: p.
    Summary: Instructions for making projects which are
modeled on museum artifacts.
    1. Handicraft—Juvenile literature. 2. Museums—
Juvenile literature. [1. Handicraft] I. Pugh, Anna,
ill. II. Title.
TT160.F56 1986   745.5   86-45532
ISBN 0-87923-645-0 (soft)

First edition
Printed in Hong Kong

It was a cold wet afternoon. Easter was two weeks away and the subject of presents was of prime concern. In an impatient effort to demonstrate to the children that thoughtful presents with an element of surprise give a lot more pleasure than the inevitable bars of soap and boxes of chocolates I marched them off to see a Russian Imperial Easter Egg. Luckily the attention of most little girls is easily captivated by any story about a princess, but on this occasion fantasy was to become a glittering reality and the children were delighted by Fabergé's creation. After the museum we went shopping but not to buy cucumber soap for Aunt Biddy or violet creams for the Grandparents. Instead we bought remnants of bright coloured silk, sparkling sequins and tiny pearls, then stopped at the butcher's for a small bag of sawdust. We had decided to make our own jewelled eggs.

Our Easter Eggs, although not perhaps to the standard that the Russian Imperial family would have expected, were greatly appreciated and what was more important the project had provided a great deal of amusement on a cold wet afternoon.

Encouraged by the children's enthusiasm and the grown-ups' appreciation I embarked on my 'Rainy Days' collection. In order to qualify, each subject had to have enough history to stimulate a visit to the museum, art gallery or historic house, and each artifact something about it which would inspire a project that could be quickly completed at home afterwards with no hint of boredom and maximum creative satisfaction. Incidentally nothing could be more boring than to finish a jewelled egg and wish you had made a pin-cushion, or to sew up a patchwork cushion and wish you had made a quilt – so please look at the special supplement at the back of the book before embarking on any particular project.

Without Anna's enchanting drawings, without the children's amusing ideas and honest criticism, without the unfailing support and constant encouragement of my bossy friends I would never have produced the book. I hope that other children, their parents, godparents, grandparents and guardians may get as much pleasure in using the book as I did in putting it together.

MF EASTER 1983

Contents

Historical sketches and project pages in alphabetical order

APRONS

'And they sewed fig leaves together, and made themselves aprons.'   GENESIS CHAPTER 3   KING JAMES' VERSION

It could be said that Adam and Eve were the first to wear a form of apron. But not until the time of Alexander the Great did aprons come into general use as a practical protection for the body and not until the seventeenth century did the decorative apron make its first appearance when, with an abundance of lace, ribbons and embroidery, it became a part of the elaborate costume of the period.

Meanwhile the different variations of the more practical apron had progressed to the extent that they provided as much of a clue to the wearer's trade as the tools he carried. Barbers were nick-named 'the checkered apron men' after their distinctive patterned apron, the water-seller was protected from any spillage and splashes by two panels of towel joined at the shoulders, the cobbler wore a shield of peaked leather to protect him from the sharp tools and black wax of his trade, while the lamp lighter wore a simple swathed affair which, while allowing him to climb a ladder safely, still protected him from any drips.

At the end of the eighteenth century the fashion for an apron which was both practical and decorative was led by Marie Antoinette. Her favourite retreat was the dairy at Rambouillet, where she would indulge herself with large dollops of fresh cream – protecting her exquisite dresses from any tell-tale spots with a long frilled and pocketed apron – not unlike the one worn by Alice, a hundred years later, for her adventures in Wonderland.

The pottery 'Snake Goddess', *which survived the destruction of a Minoan palace in c 1600* BC, *recorded the modest apron and lavish amount of make-up fashionable at the time.*

'The Dairywoman', an illustration printed c 1810, gives a clearer impression of the more practical aspect of an apron.

My rest you'd disturb early in the morn,
Leave me in bed comfortless and forlorn
Milk and water will not with me agree,
Therefore I'll nothing have to do with th...

AN APRON – PRETTY & PRACTICAL

First take measurements (see step 1)
Then you will need
Material for step 1
Matching thread
½" wide bias binding (steps 6, 9)
½" wide straight tape (step 7)
¼" wide elastic (step 8)
Sewing things must include big scissors and pinking shears, tailor's chalk, and tape measure.

NB A grown-up with a machine and who enjoys sewing can make the apron in a couple of hours–perhaps you could swap a task!

1 Take and note the following measurements
A Center neck to hemline
B Center neck to chest
C Center neck to wrist with arm outstretched
D Half the measurement of C
E Round the widest part of the head divided roughly by six
Double the A measurement to get the length of material you will need, and the C measurement for the width.

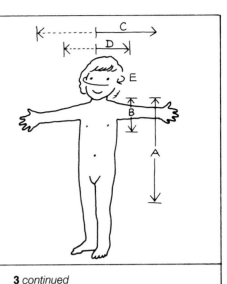

2 Fold material in half with selvages together opposite fold. Fold in half again, keeping selvages together and with the cut ends at the bottom and the folds at the top. Lie on flat surface.

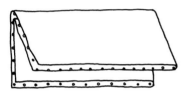

3 With tailor's chalk, mark out and join up the measurements, taking these from the folded side of the materials unless otherwise directed.
A should correspond with top folded edge to bottom cut edges.

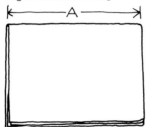

3 *continued*
B Mark this measurement down each side from the top corners. Rule across from mark to mark.

3 *continued*
C Mark this measurement along the ruled line and again along the top of the material. Rule down from mark to mark.

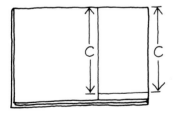

3 *continued*
D Mark this measurement along the horizontal ruled line. Now in order to shape the skirt and give it some fullness add 4 inches to the D measurement– mark this along the bottom. Rule from this mark to the original D measurement.

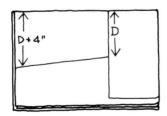

3 *continued*
E Mark this measurement along the top and down the side of the folded corners. With the chalk tied to a piece of cotton pinned to the corner, join the marks into a semi-circle.

4 Cut it out.

5 Unfold it once. Tack and then sew up the sides and under the arms. Pink the seams and press them flat.

6 Bind the raw edges of the neck, cuffs, and hem with bias binding.

7 Sewing ¾ inch in from the edge of the cuff tack, stitch the straight tape around the sleeve.

8 Measure two pieces of unstretched elastic to fit the wrist including ⅜ inch for the join. Cut and thread through the wrist tapes. Join, tuck in, and neatly sew down the tape ends.

9 With the leftovers make and bind a pocket. Don't stitch it on yet.

10 Put the apron on so that you can decide on the best position for the pocket. Sew this down in a neat stitch that won't show.

MARBLED PAPERS

'The Turks have a pretty art of chamoletting paper . . .' FRANCIS BACON 1627

A seventeenth century example of Indian marbling. This detail is taken from the Deccani miniature picture 'Rustom lassoing wild horses' *and is signed* 'The Work of Shafi'.

. . . So observed an English Lord Chancellor in the seventeenth century. He then went on to describe the manner in which paint was floated on the water and then transferred to paper so that it became 'Waived and veined like chamolet or marble'. The technique was originally used in Persia, where it was invented, in the sixteenth century.

It was supposedly an English Chancellor of the Exchequer, a century later, who was indirectly responsible for the ingenious way in which marbled papers first came to England. He allegedly introduced a heavy duty on the import of paper; and in order to avoid it marbled papers were smuggled into the country via Holland, disguised as wrapping paper which was then sold, at a high price, to the bookbinders. They smoothed out the folds and reused them as end-papers on their better bindings. Whether true or not, the finest examples of marbled papers are those of the Eighteenth century.

Bookbinders would send their books to a marbling workshop so that the end papers and the edges of the cut pages could be matched in the same marbled pattern, a custom which continued well into the nineteenth century when the amateur bookbinder was encouraged to send his work to a house of Marblers: 'it will cost him only a few pence, which will be well spent in avoiding the trouble and dirt which marbling occasions'. Despite these words of advice, however, Mr Woolnagh, in his book 'The Art of Marbling' published in 1853, describes in great detail every process and variation which, if meticulously followed, could well enable a skilled amateur to become an accomplished craftsman.

The basic technique remains much the same, with different countries pursuing their own individual style, which we find reflected in the patterns and colours as we know them today. Old Dutch is recognisable by its complexity of colours, French Shell by its group of marblish islands, English Stormount by its predominate slate colour, Spanish Marble by its effect of watered silk and Light Italian by its convincing mass of tiny veins. The finest marbled papers are still being manufactured in Italy.

A MARBLED DESK SET

You will need
A ladle, a sieve, and a bucket
A small baking dish and foil
2 clean jam jars and a pair of old tights
Paper towels and a garbage bag
An ear dropper
A small packet of cold-water size and
   a small bottle of pure turpentine
Newspapers—plenty
A tube of oil paint
   in one of the following colors:
   Sap Green, Rose Madder,
   Cadmium Yellow, Phthalo Blue
A few sharpened sticks and a
   rubber band
A package of cheap drawing paper
A notebook
2 round pencils
An old tin can and glue

1 Organize everything. Spread newspaper over working surface. Stretch a piece of the tights over one of the jars, securing it with the rubber band. Line the baking dish with foil, pressing it gently into the corners and overlapping the edges. Cut drawing paper into sheets, 1½ inches smaller all around than the baking dish (keep the off-cuts).

2 Squeeze about 1½ inches of paint into the open jam jar, and, stirring slowly, add enough turpentine to give a consistency of light cream.

3 Strain it into the jar. Throw away the piece of tights.

4 Make up the size in the bucket strictly according to the instructions on the packet. Half fill the baking dish, ladling the size through the sieve.

5 With the ear dropper put a few islands of paint (two or three drops) onto the surface, about 1½ inches apart.

6 With a sharpened stick, working on the surface of the size (careful not to go below it) pull each island into swirls and whirls, joining them together. Don't overwork the design or you'll ruin it.

7 Drop a sheet of paper flat and centrally over the size. It will immediately absorb the design.

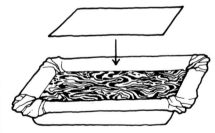

8 Spread out a few sheets of paper towels. Take the marbled paper from the size and put it face downwards on the paper towels, then turn it face upwards onto some more dry sheets.

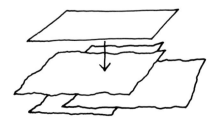

9 Clean your size by blotting off any paint around the edges with the paper off-cuts and skim across the surface. If very dirty throw out under plenty of running water and start again. Stir size with ladle before refilling the dish and marbling more sheets.

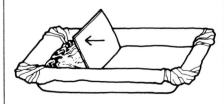

10 Once dry, use the marbled paper to cover the pencils, pencil holder (the can) and notebook.

POMANDERS

'A precious pomander to be worne against foule stinking aire' BULLEYN 1562

Pomanders became fashionable during the sixteenth century. Tree gums, herbs and essences were pounded together, rolled into a ball and carried in a box or hung in a bag from the neck or waist. Houses were draughty and people wore many layers of heavy clothing and didn't wash much, so it was wise to carry some sweet scented object to sniff when the surrounding smells got too unbearable. Herbs were also the recognised cure for most diseases and were regarded as a necessity against possible infection, so these simple objects played a demanding role in the day to day lives of our ancestors.

The earliest pomander cases were French, turned in wood, round in shape and filled with holes. Those who could afford it commissioned silver or gold cases which hung from a matching chain. All were perforated and engraved, and while some were shaped as fruit or birds others were divided into small hinged compartments, allowing the wearer a choice of fragrances such as the herbs lavender, rue or rosemary, and spices which included nutmeg, cinnamon and cloves. A simpler mixture was often concealed within a jewelled pendant or cunningly contained in the perforated knob of a gentleman's cane. Less discreet was the wooden ball which dangled among the clergyman's rosary beads; more effective was the clove-studded orange carried by Cardinal Wolsey.

In the eighteenth century a sponge impregnated with sweet smelling vinegar became the fashionable substitute for the pomander and jewellers seized the opportunity to create the most exquisite jewelled boxes. The 'vinaigrette', recognisable by its inner perforated lid, provided a handsome case for the little sponge. However, nothing retained its scent in the same way as the simple orange pomander which, having found its way to the linen cupboard, continued to outlive them all!

A Flemish pomander *made in the late sixteenth or early seventeenth century. The silver gilt ball opens to reveal a choice of six fragrances, each in its own enamelled compartment.*

A SWEET-SMELLING POMANDER

Materials required

1 thin-skinned orange,
  unbruised but juicy
1 oz cloves
* A 2 oz packet of orris root powder
1 teaspoon cinnamon powder
1 yard of ribbon not more
  than $\frac{1}{4}''$ wide, two pins
2 long strips of paper
  (same width as ribbon)
3 pieces of tissue paper
  about 12" × 12"
A small paper bag, mixing bowl,
  teaspoon, and a round metal
  skewer
* Available from most health food stores

NB Wear an apron and work
over newspaper

Will take a month to dry!

1 Cross the strips of paper, and pin them through the cross into the top of the orange.

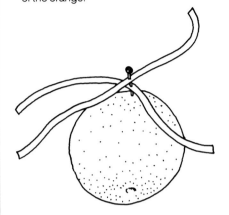

Wrap down the sides and secure with a second pin into the bottom of the orange.

2 Use the skewer to pierce a hole through the skin of the orange.

3 Push a clove gently into the hole up to its head.

4 Leaving a tiny space between the cloves, continue to first pierce and then fill each hole. Complete one section at a time, working in a regimental manner.

5 Mix the orris root and cinnamon together.

6 Remove the pins and paper strips and roll the orange in the mixture until it is totally coated, with the powder pressed firmly down between the lines of cloves.

7 Carefully place the orange on three layers of tissue paper, add any powder left in the bowl, and roll up the orange, twisting the paper at each end. Put the package into a paper bag.

8 Put the bag into a dry, dark place. Forget about it as it must dry out for at least a month. If the orange is not allowed to dry completely it will rot!

9 Cross the two lengths of ribbon and sit the pomander in the middle. Tie the ends of one ribbon on the top of the orange. Do the same with the other ribbon.

10 Make a bow with the ones you have just tied, and knot the other two ends to make a loop.

GINGERBREAD

'She don't yet know her letters – but I will bring her the ABC in gingerbread' SMOLLETT 1771

A gingerbread cavalier *who,*
when perfect became a treasured memento but which,
when chipped, provided a cheap fairground snack.

A boxwood mould *which stamped out*
both the letters and the necessary divisional lines.

In medieval times, gingerbread was an extravagant present, a welcome gift. Just like the real knights of the tournaments, gingerbread had its own shiny brown armour, glittering with gold studded fleur-de-lis. It was not so much a cake as a solid block of flour mixed with honey and spiced with ginger, liquorice, aniseed and cinnamon. Once cooked it was rubbery and didn't taste very good, but when polished with egg-white and decorated with gold-headed cloves, its appearance was irresistible. At St. Bartholomew's Fair, first held at Smithfield in the twelfth century, the gingerbread stall was always a great favourite. The most sought after souvenirs were eatable dolls in the form of the heroes and villains of the day. When the Fair finally closed after some seven hundred years of trading, the gingerbread stall was the very last to be packed up and taken home.

By the nineteenth century, gingerbread not only looked delicious but must also have tasted delicious, as the bakers had established a successful trade with gingerbread alphabets. Easily divided, these blocks of biscuits were hugely popular with small children who, once they had learnt their letters, were permitted to eat them! Yes, children were bribed into learning their letters, just as Hansel and Gretel had been lured to visit the wicked witch by her house of gingerbread, in the fairy tale first told in Germany, the land of honeycake and gingerbread, where feast days and festivals were established occasions for both gingerbread baker and wood carver to demonstrate their respective talents. The gingerbread mixture was pressed into a prepared wooden mould, so the gifted woodcarver was able to reproduce quite complicated shapes, while the baker, who was more skilled in the kitchen than in the carpentry shop, preferred to decorate simpler shapes. A good example is the brightly iced gingerbread heart which still continues to be an inexpensive gift or amusing souvenir.

MAMA COLLINS'S GINGERBREAD

Ingredients
1½ lbs plain flour
1 lb molasses
6 oz soft butter
4 oz soft brown sugar
1 oz ground ginger
½ teaspoon ground mace
An egg white
A drum of gold cake balls

You will also need
Weighing scales and sieve
Mixing bowl and wooden spoon
Pastry board and rolling pin
Biscuit cutter and baking tray
Waxed paper and wire rack
A palette knife and an ordinary one
A skewer and a paintbrush

Wear an apron
and get permission to use the oven.

1 Weigh the ingredients.
Leave the jar of molasses to stand in a bowl of hot water, which will make it runnier and easier to use.

2 Cut the butter into small chunks and put in the mixing bowl.
Sieve the flour over the butter.

3 With cold hands lightly rub butter and flour between your fingertips until the mixture looks like breadcrumbs.

4 Add the ginger and mace to the sugar and stir them into the mixture, then make a well in the middle and pour in the molasses.

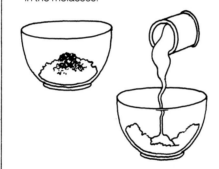

5 Stir the mixture, which is very hard work, until it comes away from the sides of the bowl. You will then have a ball of uncooked gingerbread.

6 Heat the oven to 250°. Flour the pastry board but not the rolling pin and roll out the ball of gingerbread lightly and evenly until it is as thin as a cookie.

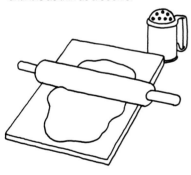

7 Line the baking tray with a sheet of waxed paper. Flour the sharp edge of the cutter and press it firmly through the gingerbread.

8 Use the palette knife to transfer the gingerbread man in the cutter to the baking tray. Remove the cutter. Make another and another . . .

9 With the skewer, make holes to hold the gold balls and marks to make the gingerbread man look more interesting. Cook in the middle of the oven for half an hour.

10 When cooked, leave the gingerbread to cool on the wire rack.
When cold, stick on the gold balls with a blob of eggwhite on the top of the paintbrush.

MONEY BOXES

'No boy ever became great as a man who did not in his youth learn to save money.'   JOHN WANAMAKER

It is thought that the peoples of Asia Minor were the first to use coins and it is from that part of the world that the earliest money box survives.

As the use of coins spread across the world so did the urge to save them. Hollow balls of flint or simple moulded shapes of clay provide most of the earliest examples. Imagine the excitement of the archaeologist on realising that the miniature glazed pottery chest he had found, decorated with a nodding bear and with a narrow hole in its lid, was a mechanical money box unearthed for the first time since it was made during the Min Dynasty. Or the amazement of the schoolboy who kicked what he thought to be a stone and out tumbled gold coins dating back to the first century BC!

The earliest wooden money boxes, used by the church in the twelfth century, were made from simple tree trunks bound with iron straps and often secured with as many as three locks – the priest would keep one key and two worthy parishoners would be entrusted with the others. A church provided a suitable setting to encourage generosity. All through Advent boxes were filled for the needy of the parish, but not opened and distributed until the day after Christmas which, as a result, became known as Boxing Day.

It was in the seventeenth century that the simple brown earthenware pig made its first appearance as a money box. Not until two centuries later, when it was possible to deposit just one penny in a savings account, did the miniature metal bank duly inscribed 'Penny Bank' become a popular alternative to the estabished 'Piggy Bank'.

Finally, more than three centuries after its original conception in pottery, the mechanical money box, cast in iron, was produced in America with a choice of characters who responded encouragingly to the gift of a coin.

An American mechanical money box *made in 1886. The mechanism is activated by pushing a coin into Uncle Sam's hand, whereupon his beard wobbles in appreciation as he drops the money into the opening bag.*

The ball of flint and Roman coins found by a schoolboy in the Chute Forest in 1927.

MATTHEW'S SECRET MONEY BOX

Materials required

Roll of parcel string (choose one with a good re-usable label)
Glue for non-porous surfaces
Scotch tape
Pencil and scissors
Can opener
A piece of card
An empty can
A ruler or tape measure

1 Completely remove the bottom of the can before washing and drying it thoroughly.

2 Cut two circles of card to fit the ends of the tin.

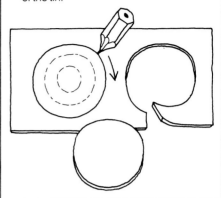

3 On one circle carefully measure and cut a slot in the center—allowing enough room for the biggest coin you hope to save.

4 With short lengths of Scotch tape, secure the slotted card to the top . . . and the plain card to the bottom of the can.

5 Cut a piece of card the same height and circumference as the can. Wrap round and secure with the tape.

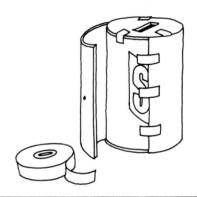

6 Turn the can upside down and spread a layer of glue on the bottom. Starting from the center, coil the string round and round, pressing it firmly onto the card.

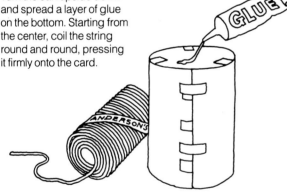

7 Turn the can right side up and work up the side, applying first a thin layer of glue, then a round of string until you reach the top.

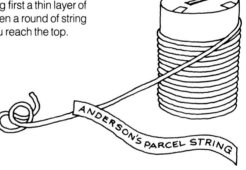

8 Continue around the top of the can. Stick down about three circles of string, ending with the string slightly to the right of the slot.

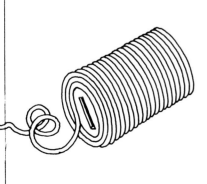

9 Continue to coil the string from the outside toward the middle within the space to the right of the slot. Do the other side in the same manner.

10 To complete the camouflage, replace the label from the original roll of string.

PAPIER MACHE

Papier mâché originated in the Orient where it was first used for making real suits of armour and lightweight theatrical masks. We know from its name that it came to England from France, where in the seventeenth century exquisite snuff boxes and elaborate picture frames were made in this material.

It was the English who, in the eighteenth century, perfected a process which put the material to its most practical use. Paper was boiled to a pulp, mixed with chalk and glue, poured or pressed into moulds and then baked or left to dry. The result was a light but strong material ideally suited to moulding the ornate ceiling decorations and wall panels of the Georgian periods.

An alternative process was developed by a printer who discovered that, by the use of heat, several sheets of specially prepared pasted paper could be sealed together, resulting in a material which was so hard that it could be treated like wood. Originally marketed as 'paperware' it was not long before it too became known as papier mâché.

Both processes provided a smooth base which, when coated with varnish and painted through a series of layers, closely resembled oriental lacquer. Its uses were many, ranging from coach panels to tea caddies, from practical mouldings to decorative furniture. But perhaps the most ambitious project was that of Messrs. Biefeld of Staines who were commissioned to build, and indeed completed, an entire village in papier mâché for a client wishing to move to Australia! Its furnishings would certainly have included items from Jennens and Betteridge, whose Birmingham firm had earlier patented a technique for the decoration of papier mâché. And it may well have been their very beautiful tea trays, inlaid with pearl shell, that led to the popularity of papier mâché during the Victorian period.

The Demon Prince Ravana. *A gilded Siamese mask made in papier mâché with teeth in mother of pearl and a head-dress set with fragments of mirror.*

You will need
A soup bowl and dinner plate
Scotch tape and modeling clay
2 newspapers
Scissors and a sheet of card
Poster paints and paintbrush
Length of ribbon or tape
Cloth or piece of rag
Mixing bowl and shallow dish
Blunt knife and wooden spoon
Cup for measuring
4 cups of flour
1 cup of water
A walnut
A carrot or parsnip
 (if unavailable use modeling clay)
NB Start a week before Halloween

Use one newspaper to protect the
working surface.
The addition of glitter or gold stars
sprinkled or stuck around the hat
is very effective.

1 The Mask Mold.
Turn the soup bowl upside down. Use
modeling clay to shape the mouth and
eyebrows and to secure the carrot firmly
in the nose position. Crack the walnut
exactly in half. Using modeling clay, stick
each half on either side of the nose for
eyes.

2 The Hat Mold.
Make a cone of card. Scotch tape it
together and secure it firmly with
modeling clay to the inner rim of the
upside-down dinner plate.

3 Cut the newspaper into strips ¾ inch
wide. Draw some of these through a
saucer of water and cover molds with
one layer of wet strips.

4 Make the paste. Put the flour into a
mixing bowl and add enough water,
from your measured cupful, to make
a smooth paste, then gradually stir
in the rest of the water.

5 One by one draw the rest of the strips
through the paste and press them
onto the molds. Use shorter pieces
to go around the tricky corners. Make
sure there are no air bubbles and
use a rag to blot off any excess moisture.
Go around and around, in the same
direction, until you have added six layers.

6 Leave to dry thoroughly in a warm place
for a couple of days.

7 Separate the papier mâché from the
molds by easing them apart carefully
with a blunt knife.

8 Cut holes in the center of the eyes.
Then make holes on either side of the
face for tapes to tie on the mask.

9 Cover the mask and hat with a good
layer of poster paint and let this
dry before you finish painting them.

AND LAST OF ALL

10 Cut the tape in half, knot the ends
and thread them through the holes on
either side—leave the ends to
resemble sticking-out ears. Take some
leftover strips of paper, paint them,
and when dry, tape them inside
the rim of the hat.
This spooky hair will complete
your halloween disguise.

MOSAICS

'Within this palis of prise was a proude halle . . . A flore that was fret all of fyne stones . . . Made after musyke, men on to loke' C 1400 ANON

The Greeks created mosaics in 400BC, pavements of black and white pebbles sunk in cement. The different tones created an impressive pattern but the irregular shapes provided an uneasy surface on which to walk. Experiments with stone and marble, cut into cubes and evenly laid resulted in mosaic pavements much as we know them today.

Although earliest examples in England date back to the second century, it was not until the end of the third century, that mosaic floors became the socially competitive feature of the Roman Villa. Agriculture produced great wealth and landowners built new homes. Most important was the dining room floor, carefully sited so that it could easily be admired by visiting merchants and envious neighbours! Mosaic pattern books were available but the richer landowners preferred to order an exclusive design of some particular mythological scene which took their fancy. Mosaicists obtained sandstone, shale, marble and limestone, cut into manageable sizes from the local stonemason. These naturally-coloured chunks were recut into small cubes and embedded into a series of marked-out panels which were then transported to the site where the floor was completed.

It was during the Middle Ages that the Italians perfected the use of mosaics in mural decoration. Whereas with pavements an uneven surface had been a disadvantage and glass cubes had proved too fragile, now both drawbacks became important features of the mosaicists art. Glass cubes, backed with colour or sandwiched with gold, were angled among the other cubes, to reflect the light. Interiors were transformed in this manner and when, during the seventeenth century, it was feared that the festivities in St. Mark's Square were disturbing the dazzling mosaics in the Cathedral, both gun salutes and fireworks were promptly banned!

Salome *from a scene which decorates the walls of the Baptistry in St. Mark's Cathedral, Venice.*

Medusa *who dominates the pattern of mosaics on the floor of the resting room in the Roman Villa at Bignor, Sussex.*

You will need

Piece of paper 6″ square

1 piece of plywood $\frac{3}{4}$″ thick × 6$\frac{1}{4}$″ square

4 lengths of thin wooden strips $\frac{1}{2}$″ broad × 6$\frac{1}{2}$″ long

Panel pins

Wood stain

Suitable brush and cleaner

* Sheet of glazed multicolored mosaic tiles $\frac{3}{8}$″ square

Tile adhesive

Tile grouting

Cloth

Different colored counters, 6 of each: buttons, beans or . . .

* Can be bought at any ceramic tile store.

1 Make up the frame. Gently hammer three panel pins into position along the bottom half of the four lengths of thin wooden strips. With one corner square and the bottom edge level, one by one, hammer these into the sides of the plywood to provide a trough on top. Paint with stain and leave to dry.

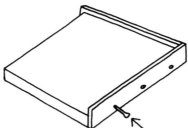

2 Peel the tiles from the mesh backing. Sort them into lines of colors. You will need 7 different colors:

48 in color A

40 in color B

32 in color C

24 in color D

16 in color E

5 in color F

4 in color G

Label the lines with the corresponding letters.

3 Rule across the paper from top to bottom and side to side. Place a tile in color F in the center. Surround this with tiles in color B.

4 Put a tile in color D in the middle of the top, bottom and either side.

5 Put a tile in color A on each side of these and complete the square with a tile in color E at each corner. These 25 tiles form one unit.

6 Start the four corner units by first extending the central unit with a tile in color A at the sides of each of the corner tiles.

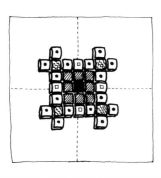

7 Complete four corner units in the same pattern as the central unit. Complete the border in between each corner unit with tiles in colors ADA.

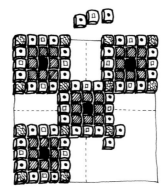

8 Finally, fill in the four remaining squares with one tile in color G surrounded by eight tiles in color C.

9 Transfer the tiles to the wooden frame. Put a blob of adhesive on the bottom of a corner tile and stick it in place. Complete a line down and a line across in the same way, leaving a tiny space between each tile. Stick down all the tiles, line by line, keeping the spaces even and the lines straight.

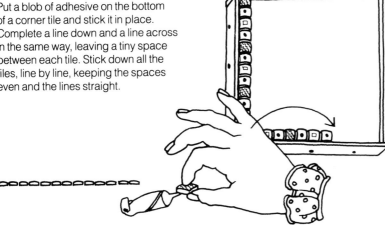

10 Grout in between the tiles. Wipe the surface with a barely damp cloth and leave the grouting to harden overnight before playing a game on the board!

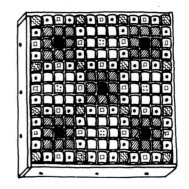

KNITTING

'In any business where the assistance of the hands is not necessary, they universally resort to knitting . . .'
GEORGE WALKER 1814

Early sculpture suggests that knitting was a craft known in the second century AD. The hand-knitting industry became established in England during the sixteenth century, when knitted caps were made, although gloves and stockings continued to be imported from Spain and Italy.

Henry VIII was painted wearing Italian hand-knitted stockings and his courtier, Lord Pembroke, is known to have ordered a pair in the finest English worsted. When Elizabeth I ascended the throne her silk stockings were knitted at court. It was to the Queen, some twenty years later, that the first machine-made stockings were presented. They came from a poor country clergyman, Parson Lee, who had devised a wooden frame, capable of knitting 1000 stitches a minute, for which he sought the Royal Approval. While recognising the potential of the invention, the Queen felt obliged to safeguard the livelihood of those of her subjects whose income depended on the hand-knitting industry, and so refused to grant him a patent.

Hand-knitting continued as a means to earning a living well into the nineteenth century. Indeed the traveller William Howitt described the knitting activities in the Yorkshire dales during the 1830s in such a manner as to suggest the people did little else! Shepherds would knit while minding their sheep, neighbours knitted as they chatted by the wayside, children attended knitting schools and learnt amusing rhymes to help them with their increasing and decreasing; finally, at the end of the day, friends would 'go-a-sitting' and gather round the fireside to exchange 'knitting stories' and click their needles by the light of the smouldering peat. The week's knitting would be gathered together for market day, on which it was not unusual for a woman, laden with the basket on her head, to complete an additional pair of socks on the journey.

The Madonna of Bexterhude, *painted during the fourteenth century by Maître Bertram, depicts an excellent example of a seamless garment knitted on four needles.*

The Wensley Dale Knitters, *an engraving used by George Walker in his book 'Costume in Yorkshire' gives a charming impression of the knitting activities at the beginning of the nineteenth century.*

You will need

4 oz double knitting yarn
 (4 · 1 oz balls)
1 pair size $\frac{3}{16}$" knitting needles
240 wooden beads, $\frac{1}{4}$" size
A tapestry needle
A small crochet hook and a
 tape measure

NB The beads must have holes large enough to slide over the eye of the tapestry needle once it has been threaded with wool. Always knit in plain knitting and slip the first stitch of each row to insure that the sides of the scarf will be straight and neat.

PS For a random color effect use beads of four different colors, threading them in strict repetitive sequence, i.e.: 1234, 1234, 1234, 1234 etc.

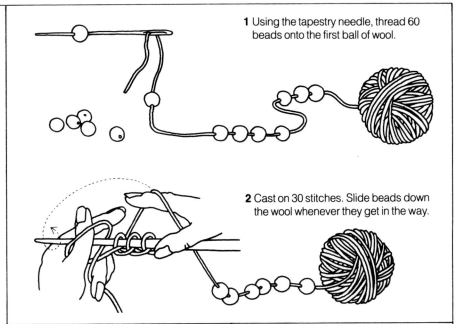

1 Using the tapestry needle, thread 60 beads onto the first ball of wool.

2 Cast on 30 stitches. Slide beads down the wool whenever they get in the way.

3 Knit three rows.

4 The fourth row is beaded. Knit five stitches, pull up a bead tight to the knitting, knit ten stitches, pull up a second bead, knit another ten stitches, pull up a third bead, knit the remaining five stitches.

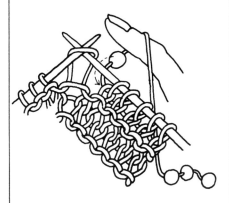

5 Knit three rows.

6 The eighth row is beaded. Knit ten stitches, pull up a bead. Knit another ten stitches, pull up a second bead. Knit the remaining ten stitches.

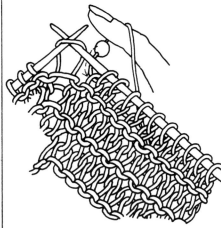

7 Knit three rows.

8 Go on repeating steps 4, 5, 6, and 7, threading more beads and joining wool when necessary. Keep back six yards of wool for tassels. Cast off after finishing step 7.

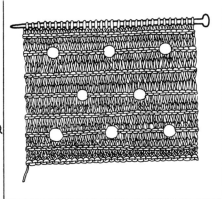

9 Cut the six yards of wool into short lengths of 4 inches. Starting next to the tail of wool on the last row of knitting, make a tassel. Loop a length of wool over the crochet hook and pull it through the first stitch, then pull the ends back through the loop. Complete a row of tassels at each end of the scarf by knotting a loop through every stitch.

10 Sew in all the loose ends— making sure that they don't show on the beaded side of the knitting.

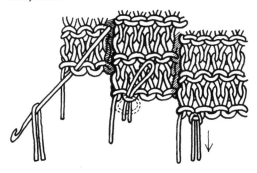

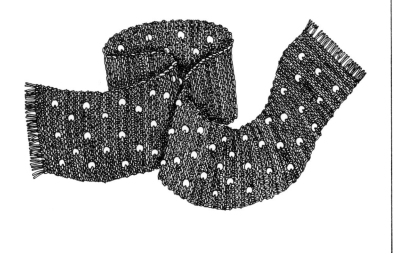

LINO-CUTS

'Linoleum that has served its term of normal life upon the floor may be equally useful . . .'   CLAUDE FLIGHT 1934

Credit for the success of linoelum must go first to Frederick Walton, the Englishman, who patented his invention in 1862. He had observed the hard crust which forms on the surface of paint exposed to the air and was sure that if this were to be dissolved in some compatible solvent it would result in a varnish, or water-proofing material, similar to india rubber. His hunch was right and after years of experiments and financial struggles Frederick Walton finally produced the most revolutionary floor covering of the late nineteenth century and, quite by chance, the most versatile illustrator's material of the early twentieth century.

As an art form linoleum, once cut and incised, lies somewhere between a woodblock and a wood engraving. As an artist's material it is very much more versatile and the tools con-siderably simpler to use than those necessary for either woodcutting or engraving. Claude Flight will be remembered as the leading exponent of lino-cuts and prints and he was responsible for the first exhibition on the subject in 1929. He taught and wrote extensively on the art, passing on tips for cutting linoleum, such as his own discovery that bodkins and filed down umbrella ribs make excellent tools. He explains the technique of cutting four blocks in order to produce a design in four colours as if it were no more complicated or inspired than that used for one block of one colour. Claude Flight felt strongly that colour lino-cuts should be available 'at a price which is equivalent to that paid by the average man for his daily beer or his cinema ticket.'

'Brooklands' by Claude Flight, 1927.

Materials required

1 piece of cork linoleum
  about 8″ × 6″, and 1 smaller piece
3 lino cutters
  in sizes two, four, and six
1 roller, 1 wooden spoon
8½″ × 11″ assorted colored paper
The top of an old cookie tin
1 tube of block paint
1 newspaper
Glue

NB Linoleum is easier to work with if left in a warm place for a couple of hours beforehand.

It is important to remember that lino-cutting is like drawing on a blackboard with chalk; each line cut will be white in the final print if printed on white paper. The image cut into the lino will be reversed in printing, so letters and numbers must be drawn on tracing paper and retraced backward directly onto the linoleum.

1 Take the small piece of linoleum—draw straight and curved lines—practice cutting them out. Hold the lino cutter with the blade almost flat, pushing the cutting edge firmly down and away from you while scooping out the line. At first the sides will be jagged, so keep practicing with the different cutters until they are all smooth.

2 Draw a simple picture on the large piece of linoleum.

3 Cut out the drawn lines, clean up the shavings.

4 Put the lino cut flat on some newspaper.

5 Squeeze a short length of paint onto the top of the cookie tin.

6 Work the roller through the paint backwards and forwards until it is evenly spread.

7 Transfer the paint. Work the roller to and fro until the raised section of lino is evenly and totally covered.

8 Make a trial print—take a piece of paper from your colored block and put it on the paint-covered lino cut, cover it with another piece of paper. Use the back of the spoon to press down—go around and around, applying even pressure—the paint will be transferred from the lino cut to the paper.

9 Take off the top layer of paper and then peel back the print. Several trials may be necessary before you get a perfect print.

10 Leave face-up to dry. Trim and stick the print on a folded sheet of matching paper.

HOOKED RAG RUGS

'I caught the fever . . . every evening I worked on the rug until it was finished' EDWARD FROST 1868

It is not known when hooked rugs were first made in England, only that originally they served a purely functional purpose. Every scrap of material, too worn for quilting and too tatty for patchwork, was hooked through coarse sacking into a solid mass of firm loops to provide a floor covering. Once dirtied by muddy shoes, fireside grime or snuggling pussy cats the 'hookie' was easily washed; when finally worn out, simply replaced. It is hardly surprising that even nineteenth century examples are fairly rare.

But in America the hooked rag rug was always primarily of decorative importance. Earliest examples date from the 1830s when simple designs outlined in charcoal were hooked through a background of homespun hemp in brightly dyed rags, features which enable the expert to pinpoint the date and locality of the rug's origin. In 1850 burlap became easily available, a canvas produced commercially with a regimented open weave, which facilitated fast and even hooking; and in the 1870s the resourceful pedlar, Edward Frost, turned his energies to the production of stencilled burlap foundations, enabling even the most uncreative to make an impressive rug for the parlour floor – a proud possession which often remained bottom up until the click of the garden gate warned of a visitor's arrival!

The most prolific years of the decorative rag rug were those of the American Civil War and the most productive years of the practical rag rug those of World Wars I and II.

A 'Hookie'. *The rug which provided a practical floor covering for day to day use.*

The Cow and Milkmaid. *A rare example of an English decorative hooked rug.*

The Lion and Beavers. *An excellent example of the American hooked rug with a bold design worked in good strong colours.*

A MINIATURE HOOKED RUG

You will need

A small piece of burlap 8″ × 10½″
A crochet hook ⅛″ size
Thin cotton remnants in
  5 contrasting colors
Pencil, ruler, and sewing things
NB Keep a square of cotton, 9″ × 6″,
uncut—it will be needed for the lining in
step 9.

1 Following the lines of weave, use a soft pencil and the ruler to mark a border on the burlap 1½ inches from the edge.

2 With a large stitch, oversew the raw edges of the burlap. Draw the outline and features of your favorite animal.

3 Cut the scraps of material into long lengths ½ inch wide.

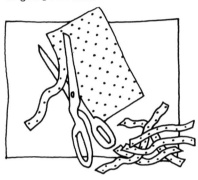

4 Practice on a spare piece of burlap. Hold a length of cotton between your fingers under the burlap. Following the holes in the weave, push the hook from above through a hole and pull up

4 *continued*
a short loop of cotton. Leave two threads of burlap, push the hook into the next hole, and pull up another loop. Do a few more until you feel confident.

5 If it does not look like this

or if you have used the wrong color, undo it by gently pulling the end of the strip of material from underneath.

6 Start the rug. Work the outline of the animal, his features, and the border in the strongest color. Then work two lines within the border in a lighter color.

7 Fill in the animal in a third color, the patch in a fourth, and the background in the fifth. It will become harder to hook evenly as the burlap gets filled with loops, so hook where you can!

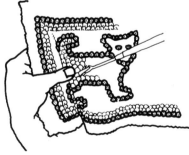

8 Once the hooking is complete, trim the edges and turn them over, securing them to the bottom of the rug with a few tacking stitches.

9 Fold in the edges of the cotton square and oversew it edge to edge over the bottom of the rug.

10 With a needle and thread, catch a few of the outside line of loops onto the backing cotton, covering up any unsightly burlap.

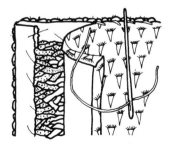

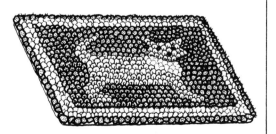

KNUCKLEBONES

. . . originally small bones from the ankle-joint of cloven-footed animals, but imitated in many different materials, were used for various games.   British Museum description.

It is over 2,000 years since the bones from the joints of a sheep were used by the Greeks as the earliest form of dice. These 'knucklebones' were either tossed in serious consultation with the gods or thrown for fun in games of skill, their four distinctive flattish sides either representing some mystic language or providing a means of scoring.

The 'astragalizontes', as the players were called, used four bones in a variety of games, the commonest of which was much the same as poker dice, with the different combinations of the uppermost flat surfaces providing the score. But whereas in poker dice the highest throw is achieved with all the dice showing the same face (i.e. 'Five Aces'), in knucklebones it is the opposite, as each face must be different. Indeed, in the time of the Emperor Augustus a player throwing the 'Four Vultures', four identical faces, would have been obliged to put coins into a pool which could be scooped by the next player to throw a 'Venus', four different faces.

Another variation of 'Knucklebones', which has been described as 'essentially a woman's game', was simply to throw the dice up in the air and catch them on the back of the hand – a game which became more painful as the centuries went by and knucklebones were cast in bronze or carved from agate, onyx and crystal. During the seventeenth century ivory replicas were popular, and it was at about that time that a ball was introduced to the game; thus the most complicated variation of knucklebones, known as 'jacks', was first conceived. However, the simpler forms persisted, acquiring in England alternative names such as 'huckle-bones' or 'dibs', depending on the part of the country where they were played.

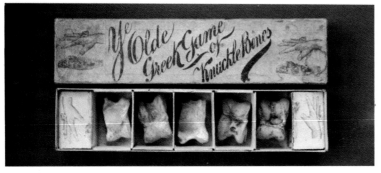

The Astragalus Players, *a marble frieze from Pompeii, which shows the game in progress during the first century* A D. *It would appear that two sets of knucklebones are being used.*

A boxed game, *bought from Whiteleys in Westbourne Grove, at the beginning of the twentieth century. Sadly, the rules are missing so the presence of a fifth knucklebone remains a mystery.*

THREE SETS OF KNUCKLEBONES

You will need
3 oz plain flour
1 oz salt
1 oz cold water
1 tsp of glycerine
Spoon and mixing bowl
Pastry board, knife, and wire tray

Special notes
There is a huge temptation to dry the modeling dough quickly in the oven. Don't, as it tends to become puffy and the knucklebones must remain absolutely flat on all four sides.

1 Mix the flour and salt together. Add the glycerine to the water and stir gradually into the dry ingredients until the dough comes cleanly away from the sides of the bowl.

2 Work the dough with your fingers on the board until it is really smooth. Roll into a sausage shape approximately 1½ inches wide and exactly 4¾ inches long. Mark into 12.

3 Cut off one length and model it until you have made an interesting shape with four flat sides. Then cut and model the remaining 11 pieces.

4 Mark one long indented line with a skewer on the uppermost side of each piece.

5 Turn the twelve pieces onto the second side and pierce three holes in a neat line.

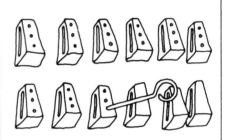

6 Turn the twelve pieces onto the third side and mark with four lines in a row.

7 Turn the twelve pieces onto the fourth side and mark with six holes in a regular pattern.

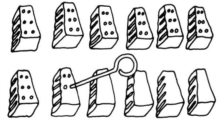

8 Put the pieces carefully on the wire tray and leave to dry for a couple of days in a warm dry place.

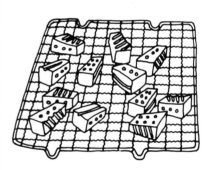

9 Make up and write out rules for a game—look at the preceding page for ideas – remember to make two extra copies for your friends.

10 Give a set of knucklebones and rules to each of two friends so that they can practice at home between games.

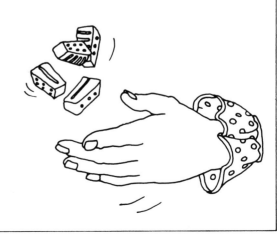

PORTABLE GARDENS

'The plants you packed in my case are all alive and healthy,
and look much fresher after the journey than many of the passengers' DR BEAUMONT 1884

In about 1825, Alan Maconochie, a Scots botanist, began experimenting to see whether grasses and ferns which grew naturally in shady damp soil would keep their bright colour if grown in an unnatural restricted atmosphere. He put a layer of peat into the bottom of an old glass container, planted some ferns and grasses and sealed the jar. The experiment was a success, so he designed and had made a tiny indoor greenhouse which sat in the window of his home filled with flourishing green plants.

At about the same time, Nathaniel Bagshaw Ward, an English doctor and naturalist at heart, had been watching a moth chrysalis which he kept with some earth in a jar. He noticed that two green shoots appeared in the soil. For years he had been trying to brighten up his gloomy London home with a series of unsuccessful plantings in his backyard. Now, fired with inspiration, he instantly set about making several glass cases which he filled with mosses and ferns. The greenery thrived and a case was duly despatched to a colleague in Australia who received the plants in perfect condition. The 'Wardian case', as it was appropriately called, was soon adopted by the Horticultural Society and by the Royal Botanical Gardens at Kew. From then on Wardian cases were used to ensure the safety of travelling specimens.

Before long Mr. Maconochie and Dr.·Ward were by no means the only people with miniature greenhouses. 'Parlour Gardening' became fashionable, reaching the height of its popularity in the middle of the nineteenth century, and it enjoys a revival today.

A fern case *made by Andrew Brown, a tinsmith and gasfitter, at the end of the nineteenth century.*

A Wardian case *carried by Dr. Beaumont, the traveller, whose letter was published in 'Cannell's Floral Guide'.*

AN INDOOR GARDEN

You will need
An airtight glass container
20 or 30 little pebbles
A small amount of garden peat
Potting compost and charcoal
*2 or 3 plants
A rolling pin and a spoon and fork
Paper for funnel, mug, and water

*Which plants will be suitable depends
on the size and shape of the container,
so take it with you when you buy the
plants, and seek advice.

Special notes
Keep the garden in a light position
but not in direct sunlight, which
would scorch the plants. Turn it every
few days so that the light is evenly
distributed. Once a month, leave the
lid off for a few hours, so the air is
changed, and cut back the plants
if necessary.

1 Put a layer of pebbles over the base
of the container.

2 Crush and sprinkle a fine layer of
charcoal over the pebbles.

3 Mix together the peat and the compost.

4 Spoon the mixture into the container
and press it evenly down with the
rolling pin. Make hollows for the plants.

5 With the spoon and fork, gently lower
the plants and their surrounding
soil into the prepared holes.

6 Push the surrounding soil firmly
down around their roots.

7 Twist a piece of paper into a funnel
and pour half a mug of water gently
down onto the soil.

8 Finally, seal the garden so that it
is airtight.

CRAVATS & BOW TIES

It was the neck cloths of Greek soldiers hired by Louis XIV in the seventeenth century, which inspired the French to introduce the cravat. Different styles were to follow, but the first was said to be named after the battle of Steinkirk in 1692. French officers, taken by surprise, had carelessly thrown on their cravats before rushing out to defeat the English. Their victory was immediately celebrated by the women of the day who, led by the famous singer Mademoiselle le Rochois, wore casually knotted cravats over their elaborate dresses. Probably much to the relief of the Prince of Orange, whose defeat had prompted the gesture, the fashion was short lived, but the cravat, tied at the front, became an alternative to the stock which, pre-arranged, was fastened at the back.

In the early nineteenth century Beau Brummel, the exquisitely dressed gambling friend of the Prince of Wales, later George IV, would spend the whole morning supervising the tying of his cravat so as to give it the most casual but uncrumpled appearance – as they creased the moment they were tied a large number were discarded before he was satisfied. Meanwhile in Paris young men were attending a course lasting six hours and costing nine francs where they learnt the basic art of tying a cravat together with a number of variations. Colours too were important. The 'American' looked its best in ocean green, the 'Irish' in cerulean blue, and while the 'Trone d'Amour' could be matched to suit the eyes of a particular young lady, the 'Ball Room' was only ever to be worn in the purest and most brilliant white.

As early as 1864 the patents office records the application for a 'made-up' bow tie, it was at about this time that the conventional hanging tie first appeared.

Bertrand Andrieu, *painted by Delafontaine, wearing a casually tied cravat.*

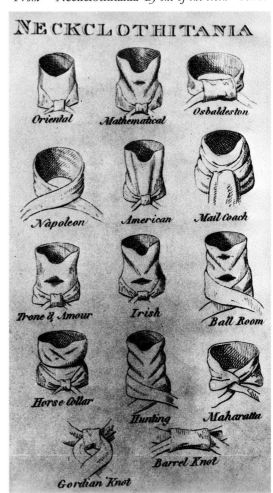

From "'Neckclothitania' By one of the cloth" 1818.

You will need
Enough material for step 1
A length of elastic
Knitting needle, scissors, sewing
    things, and
    permission to use the iron

1 From the material cut:
two pieces 4 inches × 5½ inches
two pieces 4 inches × 4¾ inches
one strip 4 inches × 1¼ inches

At this stage also cut a length of elastic to fit around the neck.

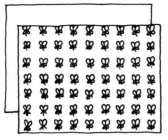 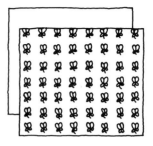 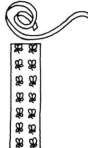

2 Take the two longer pieces and, with the right sides of the material face to face, tack them together, sewing well in from the edge.

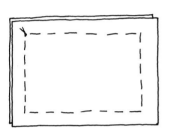

3 Now sew the pieces together in backstitch. Start on a long side, ⅜ inch in from the edge and 1½ inches in from the corner. Sew right around, finishing 1½ inches after the last corner.

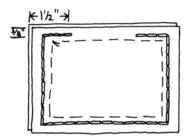

4 Carefully snip across the corners, cutting off the excess material. Take out the tacking and iron open the seams.

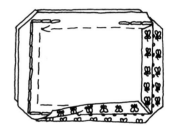

5 Pull the material the right way out through the gap left at the top. Poke the corners out gently with the knitting needle.

6 Sew up the gap with a blind stitch. Now sew the two smaller pieces together in the same way and turn them right side out.

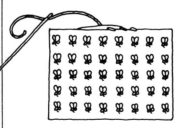

7 Find the center of the long side of the longest piece and use a running stitch to gather it from top to bottom. Do the same with the smaller piece.

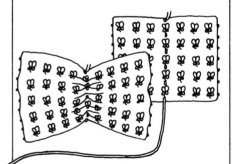

8 Sew the two pieces together with a series of running stitches, securing the gathering at the same time.

9 Fold in the long side of the strip about ¼ inch each side. Pin over the gathers, stitching the ends neatly at the back. Remove the pins.

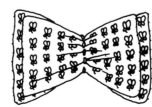

10 Thread elastic through the band at the back. Stitch the ends and hide the join under the band!

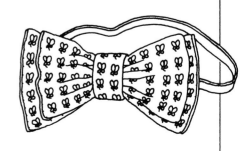

WEATHERVANES & WHIRLIGIGS

'. . . honest Balt did sit . . . watching the achievements of a little wooden warrior who, armed with a sword in each hand, was most valiantly fighting with the wind on the pinnacle of the barn.'

WASHINGTON IRVING, 'The Legend of Sleepy Hollow' 1819

The earliest weathervane, the Tower of the Winds, was erected in Athens during the first century BC. Built at a time when the winds were regarded as prophets and worshipped accordingly, it is an extraordinary feat of design and ingenuity on the part of the Greek astronomer, Andronicus.

The windvane was introduced during the ninth century, when the symbolic rooster, ordered by papal decree to 'fly' from every church steeple in Europe, served not merely to indicate the direction of the wind but primarily to provide a constant reminder of the strength and goodwill of the church. A very different attitude from that of the pope's prevailed in thirteenth century England when the heraldic windvane, which could only be flown by royal licence, turned on the turrets of stately homes, not from any interest in the weather, but as a declaration of proud ownership.

The Americans, more welcoming and less snobbish, not only established elaborate architectural windvanes but delighted in designing the homemade whirligig. Carved on many a verandah throughout the nineteenth century, its friendly presence provided an interesting topic of conversation, though people were more likely to remark on the noise it made as it turned than on the direction of the wind which turned it.

It was as much the movement as the sound that attracted children, and the popularity of the toy windmill has been recorded by writers and painters throughout the centuries. One little girl, a fourteenth century Bavarian princess, actually possessed a toy windmill made in gold and studded with pearls. She may have been an exceptionally fortunate child but the simpler version probably worked more efficiently. Often depicted by artists, it consisted of a long stick with propellers, made either in paper or material, and worked on much the same principle as the real windmill, said to have been an Arab invention of the tenth century. The design of the toy windmill has changed little over the years.

The Witch on a Broomstick, *an American whirligig made in New England during the nineteenth century.*

You will need
One packet of gummed 6″ × 6″
   colored paper squares
18″ × 24″ sheet of card
12 short bamboo sticks
* 12 metal cooking skewers, each 4″
12 small and 12 larger wooden beads
A hole puncher, kitchen sponge and dry
   cloth, pencil, ruler, scissors, and pliers
A few old matchsticks
2 or 3 yards of narrow ribbon
   and several old newspapers
* Large, long, and straight hairpins bent
   into shape provide an easily available
   alternative

1 Rule off and cut the card into twelve
squares 6 inches × 6 inches to fit the
gummed squares exactly.

2 Lie a gummed square, colored side
down, on a sheet of newspaper. Go
lightly over the gummed surface with
a damp sponge and stick a card
squarely on top.

3 Turn it over onto a sheet of dry
newspaper and rub the colored
surface smooth with a dry cloth.

4 In the same way, stick a contrasting
colored gummed square on the
other side of the card.

5 Rule from corner to corner. Mark 1 inch
from the center along each
line with an X. Then make a dot ½ inch
from each corner, ¼ inch in from the edge.

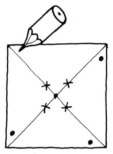

6 Cut along the lines as far as the X's.
Punch holes over the dots at each
corner and finally one in the center.

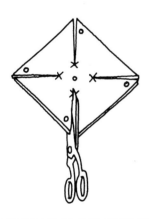

7 Thread a small bead on the skewer.
Then thread the skewer through a
corner hole from the back of the card.
Work clockwise, threading on
the remaining three corners. Finally, push
the skewer through the center hole.

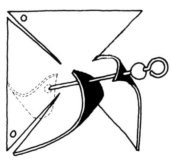

8 Thread a larger bead on the skewer
and then, with the pliers, turn it down
in a right-angle bend.

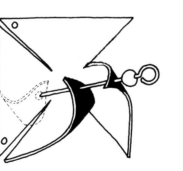

9 Push the end of the skewer into the
bamboo stick, wedging it with a
trimmed match if necessary.

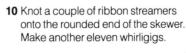

10 Knot a couple of ribbon streamers
onto the rounded end of the skewer.
Make another eleven whirligigs.

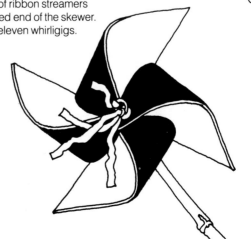

SILHOUETTES

'Profiles with gold hair drawn on them, coral earrings, blue necklaces, white frills, green dresses are ridiculous; the representation of a shade can only be executed by an outline' AUGUSTIN EDOUART 1835

A self-portrait *by Augustin Edouart cutting a silhouette of Liston the actor during the early part of the nineteenth century.*

It is to Gaius Plinius Secundas, the Roman scholar of the first century AD, commonly known as Pliny the Elder, that we are indebted for the possible origin of Profile Art. He claims it to be the invention of a Greek girl named Corinthea who, while tearfully bidding farewell to her lover, noticed his shadow on the wall. She quickly drew the outline, keeping for herself a constant reminder of her loved one, and providing her father, the potter Dibutades, with an idea for a unique form of decoration for his pots! Indeed scenes of every kind from parting lovers to fighting warriors, outlined in profile, boldly decorate most examples of early Greek pottery.

A different form of profile art became popular in France during the seventeenth century, when the side view of a head and shoulders, cut directly from a piece of paper, presented a simple form of portraiture most pockets could afford and which many people were able to do themselves. Monsieur Etienne de Silhouette, Minister of Finance during the reign of Louis XV, found this an agreeable pastime and necessary distraction from the ghastly task of saving his country from bankruptcy. Like most politicians obliged to make drastic cuts he was extremely unpopular, and when it became known that his house was hung with this cheap form of portraiture, profiles became mockingly renamed 'silhouettes'.

By the end of the eighteenth century George Washington had sat to all the leading American silhouette cutters, Mrs. Harrington had invented a complicated contraption guaranteed to reproduce an exact profile, Augustin Edouart had with his scissors alone snipped thousands of perfect 'shades' every year and Princess Elizabeth, daughter of George III, had completed a whole album of cut-out silhouettes, carefully outlining them in pencil first.

The nineteenth century saw the arrival of the camera, and the true likeness of photography resulted in the final decline of these simple portraits, which for a time remained a popular seaside novelty and a graphic means to illustrating children's books.

A family silhouette *cut by Princess Elizabeth, daughter of George III, at the beginning of the nineteenth century.*

PHOTOGRAPHIC SILHOUETTES

Materials required

A sheet of white card
A sheet of black paper
Your camera loaded with
    black-and-white film
An adjustable desk lamp fitted
    with 100-watt bulb
Good pointed scissors, string, paste,
    and a pack of white postcards
Tracing paper

Special notes

If you have one of those smart
cameras which tells you what to do—
ignore it when it tells you to use
the flash!

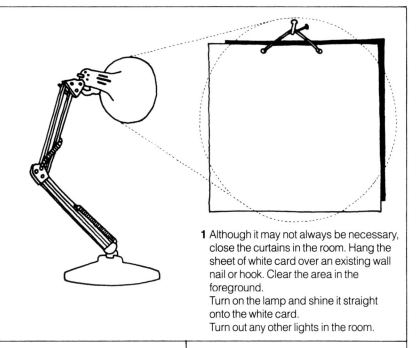

1 Although it may not always be necessary,
close the curtains in the room. Hang the
sheet of white card over an existing wall
nail or hook. Clear the area in the
foreground.
Turn on the lamp and shine it straight
onto the white card.
Turn out any other lights in the room.

2 Line up your subjects well in front of
the light between the camera and the
white card.

3 The subjects must be totally in
shadow with their most prominent
features in profile to the camera.

4 Check that the light falls only on the
background. Photograph the subjects.
Get the film off to be processed.

5 From the prints, select the best profile
of each subject.

6 Carefully and precisely cut these out.

7 Paste the cut-out profiles down onto
the white card, grouping them together.

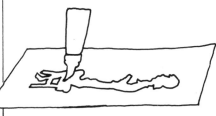

8 Trace the group, then retrace it onto
the black paper and cut it out.
Paste it onto another white card.
Use the original pasted-down print
to reproduce further copies.

APPLIQUED HANGINGS

'A trimming cut out in outline and laid on another surface.' THE OXFORD ENGLISH DICTIONARY

German vestments of the eleventh century provide the earliest examples of appliquéd work. The production of Italian velvet and French damask was responsible for the popularity of appliqué throughout Europe during the sixteenth and seventeenth centuries. Birds, flowers, heraldic emblems and religious symbols were either first embroidered on canvas, cut out, and stitched on the background, or the motif was cut from a number of different coloured materials, arranged on the background, and oversewn in position with a cord covering all the raw edges.

Many homes, particularly in England during the Tudor and Stuart periods, were dependent on tapestries and appliquéd hangings to brighten their interiors; the heavy oak panelling, exposed timber beams and sturdily carved furniture presented an otherwise gloomy atmosphere. Until the early Georgian period appliquéd work held a position of certain grandeur in the home, but then, as the classical taste of the eighteenth century was established, with fine silks and printed chintzes presenting a fashionable alternative, appliqué combined with patchwork and quilting became more romantic. While the clutter and fussiness of both Victorian and Edwardian interiors suggest a revival of appliquéd work in its original style, this was not so. Its most stable use through the centuries has always been its association with church furnishings; altar cloths, panels, vestments and canopies provide a perfect flat surface on which to work and fine examples can be seen in churches and cathedrals all over the world.

A section of an elaborate wall hanging made in Germany during the fifteenth century. It tells the tale of Tristram, the handsome hero of the middle ages who, in this scene, is shown bravely slaying a dragon.

You will need

A large old picture-frame
A piece of burlap the same size
    as the picture-frame
Paint or varnish for the frame
A piece of paper the same size as
    the opening
A packet of colored pipe cleaners
2 or 3 squares of colored felt
    including a flesh-tone
Soft embroidery threads
Some beads and sequins
Scissors and sewing things
2 dozen thumb tacks
A stencil alphabet with 2″ letters

Special notes

A gingerbread cutter provided an
excellent outline for the boy, and
magazine pictures worked well for the
other subjects.

1 Clean up and paint or varnish the frame. While it is drying, plan the picture on the paper.

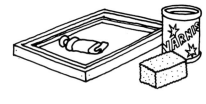

2 Once the frame is dry, cut a piece of burlap and stretch it firmly across the back of the frame, securing it first at each corner and then all around with the tacks. Make sure it is quite taut and it will provide an excellent embroidery frame.

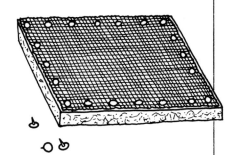

3 Cut the letters you need from the stencil alphabet, keeping close to the outline. Arrange them along the top of the picture on the paper.

4 With the picture frame right side up, transfer the letters to the burlap. One by one draw all the way around each letter with a soft pencil.

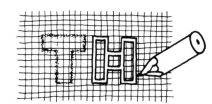

5 Take the main subjects: cut them out first in paper, then in felt. Cut more paper patterns for clothes, dog patches, etc. Pin onto scraps of material and cut out. Pin material, clothes, and patches onto the basic shapes.

6 Stitch the name on the burlap by taking a pipe cleaner and over-stitching it along the penciled line, bending it into the shape of the letter as you go. Fit the ends neatly together.

7 First pin, then tack all the motifs in position on the burlap. Cover all the raw edges with either embroidery thread or bended pipe cleaners oversewn in position.

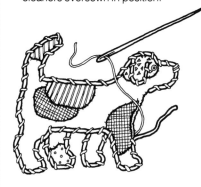

8 Finishing touches should include beads for the eyes and dog's nose, sequins on the butterflies, zigzagging of pipe cleaners for a mop of hair and a couple of bows on the kite string.

SHELLS IN DECORATION

'She knows french musick, and drawing, sews neatly, makes shellwork.' DR JOHNSON

Sculptors, painters, carvers, silversmiths and architects have throughout the centuries, been repeatedly motivated to reproduce shells in their work, yet the use of real shells in decoration remained virtually unexploited until the seventeenth century. Then the Dutch, exploiting the comings and goings of merchant vessels from all over the world, opened a central shell market where collectors were able to find rare specimens for their collections and where it was possible for architects to place orders for large quantities of common varieties.

The fountain in the gardens at Rosendael, a castle in the Netherlands restored in the eighteenth century, is a perfect example of early shell decoration set in natural surroundings. A totally different, very classical, example is the sitting room of the Shell Cottage at Rambouillet, commissioned by Louis XVI for Marie Antoinette, where shells of every variety are meticulously arranged to emphasize the architectural details.

The decoration of grottoes and follies, with embellishments of fossils and shells, became the rage in the middle of the eighteenth century. Expense seemed of little importance, in 1751 Lord Shaftesbury admitted to spending £10,000 on shells alone – perhaps not so excessive as many of the oyster shells were delivered complete with pearls! Even so, he still had the plasterer to pay, whose task of arranging and fixing the shells was long and tedious. One shell grotto, on the other hand, cost nothing, since the Duchess to whom it belonged neither bought the shells nor paid to have them installed. The shells came as gifts from her husband's admiring friends and she with her two daughters spent seven years arranging them on the walls.

By the start of the nineteenth century shellwork on a considerably smaller scale became a fashionable pastime and while Victorian women were creating pictures and ornaments, the sailors and traders of the West Indies were establishing a busy trade in shell valentines.

A privileged glimpse from the doorway of a grotto, decorated with shells during the eighteenth century, and now too fragile for visitors. BELOW: *A detail*

CAMILLA'S SHELL FRAME

Materials required
* Small flat wooden picture frame
  Selection of shells
  A tube of white glue
  Clear varnish
  Chlorine bleach
  Roll of paper towels
  Paper, pencil, and a holiday snapshot
* easily and cheaply acquired at yard sales or junk shops

NB Work over newspaper

Don't worry if you haven't got enough shells to do around the edges—it is still very pretty without them.

1 Go to the beach and collect a bucketful of assorted shells.

2 Clean the shells by soaking them for a couple of hours in a bowl of water with a spoonful of chlorine bleach.

3 Sort them out and let them drain overnight open-side down on a few sheets of paper towels.

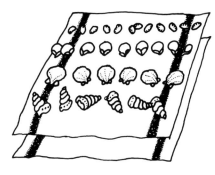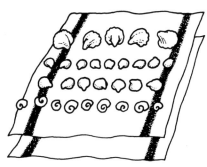

4 Put the frame on a sheet of paper; draw around the outside and inner edges.

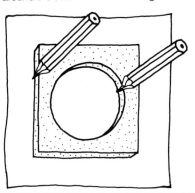

5 Use the paper frame to plan the arrangement of shells.

6 Take a shell from the pattern. Dab on a little adhesive and stick it in the corresponding position on the frame.

7 Transfer all the shells in this manner, keeping the little ones for the edges.

8 Once the glue is dry, paint with a thin layer of varnish.

STRAW MARQUETRY

'French prisoners who were confined here (Norman Cross) during the last war employed themselves in making bone toys and straw boxes . . .' CROSBY'S COMPLETE POCKET GAZETTE 1818

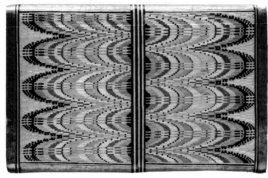

Four examples taken from an extensive collection of straw marquetry, made by French prisoners of war at the Norman Cross Camp, during the late eighteenth and early nineteenth centuries.

Straw work, of a purely decorative rather than a practical nature, was first used to make straw dolls during the seventh century BC. Born in the valley of the Nile, these very first 'corn dollies' represented a token of gratitude for a fruitful harvest from the women farmers to the goddess Isis.

It was not until the seventeenth century that the use of 'straw marquetry' was first recorded. The word 'marquetry' describes the technique employed by the German, Dutch and French cabinet makers, who used a thin layer of different coloured and grained woods, carefully shaped and butted together, to provide a decorative finish to the furniture of the period. French craftsmen were the first to realise that a similar geometric effect could be achieved with straw. Laid in alternative directions to the light, its natural colour produced a variety of shades. Moreover it was an ideal material; it bleached and dyed perfectly, it cut and split easily, once arranged and glued it cheaply transformed a simple wooden box into an ornamental casket.

It may well have been the descendants of these same French craftsmen who, among the prisoners of war in England at the end of the eighteenth century, established straw marquetry as the most popular prison pastime and an easy means to extra pocket money. The prison markets did a brisk trade in workboxes, pictures, toys and ornaments, and it was from these markets that most of the finest examples of straw marquetry originally came.

A MARQUETRY MATCHBOX

You will need

A box of wooden kitchen matches
1 sheet ¼" square graph paper
2 balls of ¼" wide shiny 'gift wrap-
   ping ribbon,' one gold and one red
A white glue stick or double-sided
   Scotch tape
Scissors, ruler, and pencil
Paintbox and paintbrush
Clear polyurethane
A suitable brush and paint thinner

Before starting the project, put the
matches safely to one side. Paint
the container to match the
background color of the outer box.

NB If using glue, work over
newspaper

1 Cut from the squared paper:
One piece 23 × 13 squares, mark it A
Two pieces 9 × 18 squares, mark them B
One piece 6 × 23 squares, mark it C
Two pieces 5 × 11 squares, mark them D
Note the diagram, as the directions
'across' and 'along' are important to
understand.

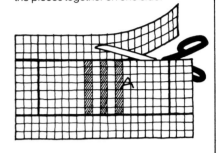

2 Take the piece marked A. Draw lines
as shown in the drawing and cut it
into five pieces. Shade in the central
line of squares on the oblong
section and, leaving one row blank,
shade in the next on either side. Put
the pieces together on one side.

3 Take the piece marked B. On the plain
side, mark the center of each long
side. Rule across. Rule up from the
point of each bottom corner to the tip
of the central line, making one large,
with two inner, triangles. Measure
diagonally and rule two lines on
either side of large triangle lines.
It's important to be accurate. Complete
the second piece B in the same way.

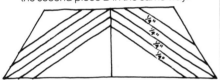

4 Turn to the squared side and mark
the center of each long side. Rule
across. On either side of the ruled
line, stick a length of red ribbon.
Then in each direction stick
alternate strips of first gold, then red
ribbon. Follow the lines—butt up the
ribbons but do not overlap. Complete
the second piece B in the same way.

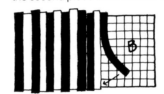

5 Turn back to the plain side. Cut up
the central line, then along the
diagonal lines of first one, then the
other triangle, keeping the strips in
separate piles. They will have
slanting bands of color on them. Complete
the second piece B in the same way,
again keeping the piles separate.

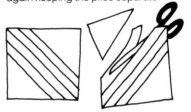

6 Take the piece marked C. Rule
along the squared surface, press
hard so that the lines show through
to the plain side. Stick a length of red
ribbon across the first row of
squares, then fill the sheet,
alternating the two colors. Turn to
the plain side and cut along the
marked lines. Keep the strips in a
separate pile. They will have
squares of color on them.

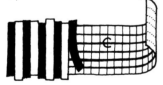

7 From the five pieces of paper, cut
from the one marked A, which will
nearly cover the top of the box, take
one of the long lengths. Stick a strip
of the colored squares along the
middle with a length of red ribbon on
either side. Cover the other long
length to match. With two lengths
of seven colored squares, keeping
gold at each end, repeat the process
on the two shorter pieces of paper.

8 Take the oblong piece left from sheet A.
Stick lengths of red ribbon across the
shaded lines of squares and fill in
between with colored squares, gold
at each end, seven squares long. Take
one set of diagonal strips made from
one of the pieces marked B and by
combining strips from each pile make
a zigzag pattern. Measure mark, trim,
cut, and stick the pattern on along one
side of the central panel and use
the second set of diagonal strips to
complete the other side.

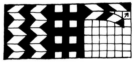

9 Take the two pieces marked D. Stick
a length of red along the middle row,
short at each end by two squares,
and then a border of red all around the
edge. Fill the space with lengths of
colored squares, keeping red in
each corner.

10 Arrange, then stick the
five pieces centrally in
position on the lid and
the two others at either
end. Seal the lid and
the outside of the
container with a coat of
polyurethane. Once
dry, replace the
matches.

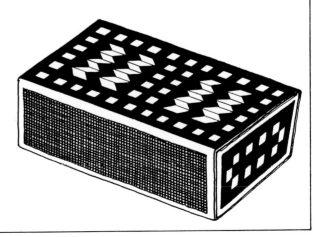

VALENTINES

'Tis yours this token to improve
Its worth depends on you,
A TRIFLE, *if you do not love,*
A TREASURE, *if you do'*

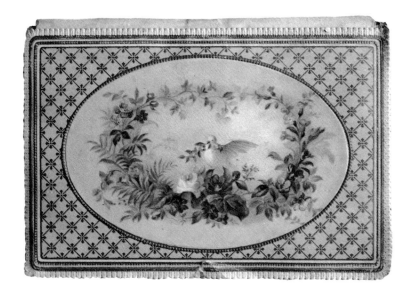

The festival of Lupercalia, held at the beginning of February, honoured the mythological gods Pan and Juno, and was the annual event at which young Romans looked forward to drawing lots for sweethearts.

This tradition continued well into the eighteenth century, by which time the romantic association was attributed to the Christian martyr, St Valentine, whose feast day is celebrated on the fourteenth of February – a date which became the accepted occasion for affairs of the heart to be taken to unusual lengths. While an innocent girl might pin bay leaves to her pillow, expecting to dream of her future husband, a more wordly young woman with a number of suitors, might have written their names on scraps of paper, wrapped them individually in clay, thrown them together in a bowl of water and chosen the first to surface. Those less superstitious, or whose fate was already decided, preferred the more traditional exchange of a gift or card. The conventional gesture was a poem, and a young man unable to compose his own verses could copy one from a selection published expressly for the purpose. In exchange he hoped to receive a handmade card with some romantic illustration and a reassuring message. Whatever the exchanges – all were sealed with wax and delivered anonymously to the doorstep.

The nineteenth century saw the introduction of the postage stamp and the commercial heyday of the valentine card. While embossed blank cards with fancy paper lace borders encouraged the enclosure of pressed flowers, scented sachets and personal inscriptions, the selection of artistic, humorous and mechanical cards, printed and ready to post, meant such an important choice could safely be left to the last minute, and still arrive in time.

Just as the sender of this enchanting valentine card remains anonymous, so does its date. In the first illustration we see the card as it would appear direct from its envelope – an almost disappointing gesture for such an important occasion. But a surprise is in store and in the second illustration the card is shown open to reveal a dazzling theatrical set with the characters of Romeo and Juliet suitably cast to provide a romantic message.

You will need
A packet of scarlet tissue paper
3 sheets of $\frac{1}{4}$" square graph paper
Good paper scissors
Pencil
White paste
A piece of white card 8" × 6"
  folded vertically and envelope
  to fit and a red pen

1 Cut three pieces of graph paper 44 squares by 28 squares. Fold each sheet in half vertically. Cut off the bottom right-hand corner of each and mark the sheets A, B, and C.

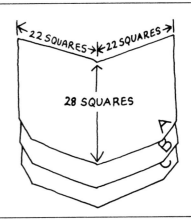

2 Make two stencils. Take sheet A. Count 16 squares across, then 7 squares down, and shade in the 8th. Repeat all the way down, leaving the last 4 squares. Shade along the lines where there is already a shaded square toward the folds on the left.

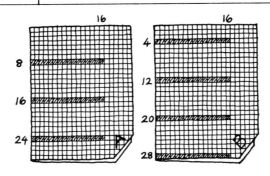

2 *continued*
Take sheet B. Count 16 squares across, then 3 squares down, and shade in the 4th. Count 7 squares down and shade in the 8th, continue shading every 8th square including the bottom line. Again, shade along the lines to the folds on the left. Cut the shaded lines of squares out of both sheets.

3 Take the folded tissue paper straight out of the packet. Take stencil A and lay it on top of the paper in the center. Cut carefully all the way around it.

4 Spread the paste through the three slots of the stencil onto the top sheet of tissue paper. Put the stencil to one side.

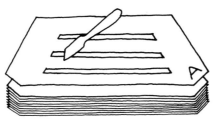

5 Take the pasted sheet of tissue paper, turn it over, and lay it squarely over the one beneath. Run your finger lightly over the pasted lines and put the joined sheets in a separate pile. Repeat the process until you have a pile of twelve pairs.

6 Now take stencil B. Put it squarely on top of the pile and repeat the process, thus pasting all the pairs together. Fold the pile in half to make a fold-line. Open again and paste through stencil B onto the top sheet. Refold and leave to dry under a heavy book.

7 Make a template. Take sheet C. Count 7 squares down along the folded edges and mark with an X. Count 16 squares across from this point and mark another X. Use the X's as guides to draw half a heart. Take the folded tissue sheets and fit them in the folded template. Cut out the heart.

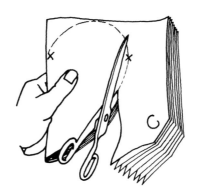

8 Paste first one side of the tissue heart, then the other into the card. Write a soppy message in red on the outside.

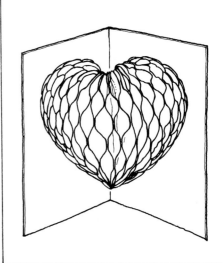

QUILTING

'So we quilted and rolled, talked and laughed, got one quilt done and put in another.'

PHOEBE EARLE GIBBONS Pennsylvania Dutch and other Essays

Made from a sandwich of cloth filled with grass or leaves, the earliest form of quilting consisted of a series of knots which held it all together. From the first century quilted materials are known to have provided a solid shield of protection against the bitter cold, hard ground and perils of the battlefield.

As the centuries progressed so did the variations of quilting; new materials and softer stuffings prompted different sewing techniques, a small line of running stitches created an agreeable pattern, extra padding emphasized the puffed effect and the insertion of cord resulted in a raised line.

During the sixteenth and seventeenth centuries quilted doublets and cuffs became an important detail of men's dress. But perhaps the most triumphant appearance of quilting was made in the middle of the eighteenth century, when the quilted petticoat, which up till then had been well hidden, became an important feature of a fashionable woman's overall appearance, with skirts opened to reveal the exquisite needlework underneath.

Meanwhile quilting in its more practical form had been established in America and by the middle of the nineteenth century most households had a set of straight topped 'quilting chairs' and a homemade 'quilting frame' – the necessary possessions required to host a 'quilting bee', a popular social occasion at which a good deal of gossip was exchanged while individually worked patchwork or appliquéd sections were first assembled then joined and quilted together. Marvellous collections of these warm and decorative quilts can be seen throughout the museums of America.

Detail from the quilted counterpane made by Virginia Ivey in 1856, showing the Fairground near Russellville, Kentucky.

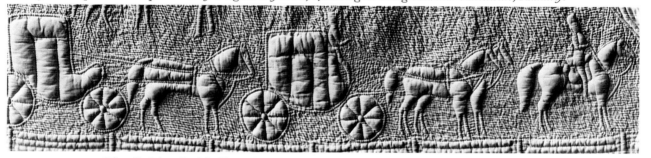

'The Quilting Bee' by Fannie Lou Spelche, 1968. An American artist has recorded a familiar scene.

Materials required
10″ of spotted cotton
10″ of 4 oz terylene wadding
39″ of narrow silk cord
A press stud
Crochet yarn and sewing things

1 Measure, rule, and cut a length of fabric $6\frac{1}{4}$ inches × $20\frac{1}{2}$ inches, using the spots as guidelines. Then measure and cut a piece of wadding $4\frac{3}{4}$ inches × 19 inches.

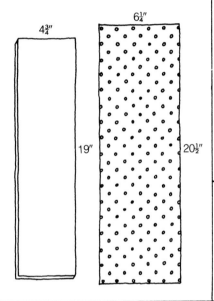

2 Mark the center of each side of both wadding and fabric. Lie the wadding over the fabric, lining up the marks.

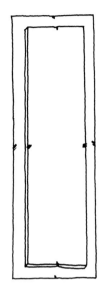

3 Work on a flat surface. Run two lines of tacking through both materials, from one mark to another. Secure with a series of diagonal tacking lines in both directions.

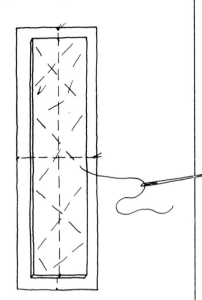

4 On the right side of the fabric, make a loose knot over the spot which is nearest to the cross of tacking stitches. This is the center.

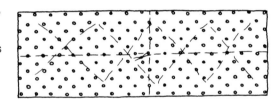

5 Start quilting. Knot a thread at the edge of the wadding and make a tiny running stitch between each spot through both materials along one of the diagonal lines which cuts through the central knot. Finish the thread at the edge of the wadding and sew the other diagonal line.

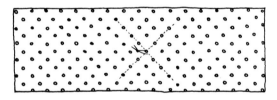

6 Leave three clear rows of diagonal spots on each side of the stitched lines, sewing along the fourth row on either side. This completes the pattern. Drawing shows stitched rows only.

7 Continue to stitch along every fourth line until the fabric is quilted with a pattern of diamonds. Remove all the tacking.

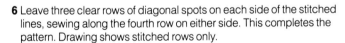
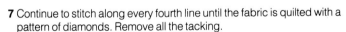
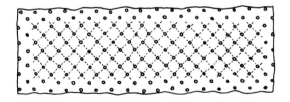

8 Tack the edges under. Make one end straight and shape the other to follow the pattern. Loosely sew any overlapping fabric to the surface of the wadding on the wrong side.

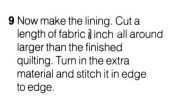

9 Now make the lining. Cut a length of fabric $\frac{3}{8}$ inch all around larger than the finished quilting. Turn in the extra material and stitch it in edge to edge.

10 Fold over 7 inches from the square end and stitch up the sides. Oversew cord around the three visible sewn edges and finally attach a snap to hold the flap when closed.

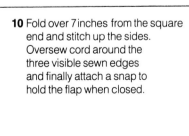

REMEMBRANCE POPPIES

'In Flanders fields the poppies grow
Between the crosses, row on row
That mark our place . . .' JOHN MCCRAE 1915

The goddess Ceres, to whom the origin of the poppy is sometimes attributed, would certainly have dismissed the legend that the vivid colour of the poppies which grew on the battlefields of Waterloo in 1815 came from the blood of the warriors. Nevertheless it was the tragic reality of a similar landscape in 1915, after the very first attack in Flanders during the First World War, which moved the Canadian medical officer, John McCrae, to write his famous poem. Perhaps the courageous resistance of the troops under General Haig during the second attack on Flanders in 1918, prompted the General to suggest that resources should be found to provide security, after the war, for the 600,000 ex-servicemen who had sacrificed so much for their country. His

resolution to provide work for the disabled and pensions for their families resulted in the birth of the British Legion in 1921. A chief source of income was to come from the sale of artificial poppies – Armistice had been signed on 11th November, 1918, so this was considered an appropriate date to launch a public appeal. The very first sales in 1921 realised £106,000. This encouraging sum persuaded the British Legion to set up their own workshops and in the following year the first workshop was opened. In 1981 the 'Poppy Factory' employed 182 ex-servicemen, many of whom were badly disabled, but who together produced 45,000,000 poppies, 200,000 crosses and 66,000 wreaths which raised £5,340,861.00.

The Somme Battlefield, pastel by Miss Oliver, recording the tragic loss of life.

The commemorative stamp issued in 1968 on the 50th anniversary of the death of John McCrae.

The Cenotaph, a first sketch by Lutyens, for the war memorial in Whitehall.

A wreath from the Poppy Factory in Richmond.

Materials required

Packets of crêpe paper in scarlet, black, and green
Scotch tape
5 twigs for stalks
Yellow embroidery thread
Scissors and ruler
10 cotton balls

Special notes

Crêpe paper comes in folded packs. Trim off the uneven first fold before embarking on the project.

1 Unfold two widths of red paper and cut along the second fold. Refold. Cut two strips 8 inches long. Fold each in half and put one on top of the other with the folds at the left and at the bottom with the grain running up and down. Measure 2 inches along the bottom from the folded corners and cut straight up $\frac{3}{8}$ inch, then turn the scissors out to the right and in a broad circle cut up and all around to the top left-hand corner. Snip off the corners.

2 Unfold two widths of black paper and cut along the second fold. Refold. Cut three strips 6 inches long. Fit them into each other like the leaves of an exercise book. Fold in half with folds at the left and at the bottom with the grain running up and down. Measure 3 inches along from the folded corners and cut a semicircle back up to the folded edges. Now cut 9 or 10 lines 1 inch long from the edge of the semicircle toward the corner, then snip off the folded corners.

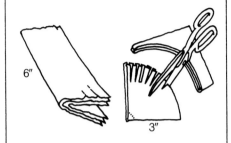

3 Unfold another two widths of black paper and cut a strip 6 inches long. Refold. Fold in half with folds at the left and at the bottom. Measure 3 inches along the bottom from the folded corners and cut a semicircle back up to the folded edges. Open up the circle.

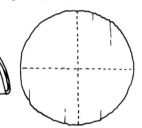

4 Take a twig. Wrap two cotton balls around the top and cover with the circle of black paper. Pull it over the cotton ball, gathering it around the base at the top of the twig. Secure with Scotch tape.

5 Tie the thread around the top of the twig, take it over the black ball and around the twig again. Repeat three times.

6 Open the black fringed circles and thread them together onto the twig. Gather the fringes around the ball and secure the surplus paper around the twig with tape.

7 Open up the red petals and with the thumb and first finger stretch the paper gently from the center outward to give the petals a natural floppy look.

8 Thread the petals onto the twig. Leave $\frac{3}{4}$ inch pleated around the twig and arrange them realistically in position before securing with tape.

9 Cut a strip $\frac{3}{4}$ inch wide from the bottom of the whole packet of green paper. Use this to bandage around the base of the flower, covering the tape. Then work down the twig. Secure at the bottom with a tiny piece of tape.

10 To complete the bunch, make four more poppies in the same way, pressing the petals more tightly together in some than in others.

SOLITAIRE

'Se joue seul. C'est une grande distraction, sans aucune fatigue, pour un malade même alité.'

REGLES DE TOUS LES JEUX

There are two popular and equally believable explanations of how the game Solitaire first came to be played. Some say that it was the conception of the French writer, Paul Pellisson, imprisoned for his political views during the seventeenth century, who adapted the traditional Fox and Geese board to provide a game of patience more suited to his solitary confinement; while others suggest that it was the invention of a French military officer whose inspiration came from the colonies, where he had observed returning huntsmen neatly replacing their arrows into a fitted case of graduated lines and regimented holes.

The Solitaire board originally had a handle and thirty seven holes. The game was played with pegs, usually made of wood, although during the eighteenth century a number of sets were produced in ivory. This was a period when the game was greatly in vogue, providing an ideal occupation or animated topic of discussion on long sea voyages and a popular pastime or point of conversation at country house parties. Mathematicians devised a variety of different combinations and the game became one of considerable skill – as well as requiring formidable patience. One variation, 'The Lecturer Surrounded by his Friends', ruled that one peg must be left isolated in the middle of twenty-one empty holes bordered with the remaining sixteen pegs; while another, 'The Cross of St Andrew', dictated that the board should be almost totally cleared, leaving only five pegs – but they must be in the correct formation.

Two centuries later, in a more up to date book of French games, the classical variation, described as 'The English Solitaire', suggested that by reducing the number of holes to thirty three the game, while retaining its original objective, would be considerably easier to play. It is this variation, all too often supplied with the solution, which is Solitaire as we know it today.

This illustration of a young lady quietly enjoying a game of solitaire is one of a number of charming illustrations from a book published in 1823, with no mention of an author, entitled 'Jeux des jeunes filles de tous pays.'

You will need
An old newspaper
A sheet of fine sandpaper
* A pack of modeling clay
* Paint and paintbrush
Drawing things including ruler, compass, and paper
36 marbles
An empty flowerpot, old tray, rolling pin, scissors, and spatula
* Choose modeling clay that requires no cooking, and use paints recommended on the packet.

1 Rule off an area of paper 8¾ inches square. Mark the center of each side and rule across with a firm line. Mark and rule a lighter line 1 inch away on either side of each line.

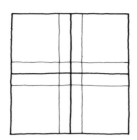

2 Set the compass with the point and pencil 3⅝ inches apart and draw a circle from the central mark. Reset it at 4 inches and draw an outer circle. Cut it out.

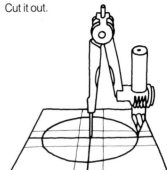

3 From the central point measure and mark 1 inch along each line. . . . Then mark where the lines cross. . . . Now measure 1 inch from the outside marks in all directions and mark again . . . do the same again.

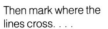

4 On the bottom of the tray roll out the clay evenly into a shape slightly larger than the paper circle, and about ¾ inch thick.

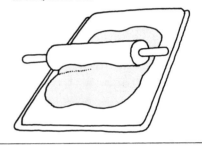

5 Pin through some of the marks to secure the paper circle over the clay. Gently pierce through the paper with the compass point, transferring the inner circle and all the marks but not the lines onto the clay.

6 Remove the paper. With the end of the pencil, slightly angled so that the excess of clay is pushed to the edge, gently and firmly make a ditch over the inner circle of pinpricks.

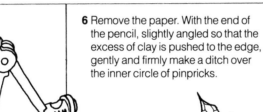
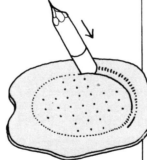

7 Press the pencil over all the marks in the center. Put a bead or marble into each hole and roll it around and around until it fits snugly.

8 Lightly reposition the paper circle over clay and cut around the outside with a knife.

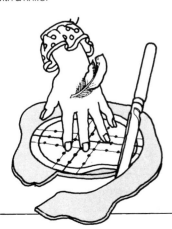

9 Cover with a folded newspaper and then the flowerpot and leave to dry in a warm place. Once the top is dry turn it over with a spatula and let it dry right through.

10 Smooth away any hairline cracks and bumps with fine sandpaper before finally painting the solitaire board.

SLIDE WHISTLES

'The required note, in any key or pitch, is obtainable simply by the movement of a slide and no adjustment or tuning is required before playing with other instruments, record players or the radio.'

BARNES & MULLINS CATALOGUE 1962

The simple whistle, whether elaborately sculpted in clay or ingeniously cast in metal, still produces only one note, whereas the slide whistle, even in its simplest form, can be controlled to play a complete scale. Earliest slide whistles were whittled from mulberry, fig, willow or other suitably hollow woods. Two straight twigs, one fat and one thin, were necessary. The fatter twig, hollowed right through was carved at one end to make a whistle. The thinner twig was carefully stripped of its bark and then wrapped round one end to make a stopper. The player then blew a tune, varying the sound by moving the stopper up and down within the long whistle. Such slide whistles were used in India to imitate bird calls, in Greece to play folk music and in more primitive countries as an accompaniment to the witch doctor's rituals.

As a serious musical instrument the 'slide whistle' remains little documented. Historians differ in their opinion as to whether it should be described as a percussion or woodwind instrument and refer one from 'slide whistle' to 'swanee whistle' with no explanation as to how it came by the name – one gets the feeling they would rather not mention it at all. Known in France as a 'sifflet à coulisse', it was in Monte Carlo in 1925 that the instrument made its first orchestral performance. Ravel scored a small part for it in the garden scene of his opera 'L'enfant et Les Sortileges'. In 1935 Gavin Gordon used a slide whistle to simulate a shaky singing voice in his Sadler's Wells production of 'The Rake's Progress'.

As a jazz instrument the 'swanee whistle' has an interesting entry in the Guinness Book of Music, but still no explanation for the name; which leads one to presume that the instrument is of American origin – not so, it's British.

In 1895, two banjo players Mr. Barnes and Mr. Mullins, moved to London where they established a firm manufacturing banjos. They had been in business for nearly twenty-five years making, wholesaling and exporting musical instruments of every variety including slide whistles made in metal and bakelite when, in 1919, the popular hit 'Swanee', with music by George Gershwin and lyrics by Irving Caesar was published. The partners, aware of the new movement in symphonic jazz and swinging dance music, simply re-registered their slide whistle with the new name of 'swanee' whistle. Paul Whiteman, with his so-called jazz orchestra, featured the instrument in his recording of 'Whispering' made in 1920. Louis Armstrong demonstrated its versatility when he put his trumpet to one side and played a solo on the swanee whistle for his record 'Woosit' made in 1926. A nice sales booster for Barnes and Mullins who have to date sold more than two million 'swanee' whistles.

The piccolo swanee whistle *which is now a museum exhibit.*

The cover of a Barnes & Mullins catalogue printed in the sixties.

An entry from an earlier catalogue showing the wide variety of swanee whistles *available in 1938.*

You will need
A length of dry bamboo 1"
  in diameter
A length of dry bamboo $\frac{3}{8}$"
  in diameter
1 wine-bottle cork
Sandpaper
2 cotton balls
Fine string or thick thread
A piece of old rag
A penknife and a hacksaw

NB Don't forget to ask permission
before using the dangerous things!

1 Saw the thick bamboo into shorter
lengths, cutting between the nodes,
to get one length of hollow bamboo
9½ inches long. Cut the narrower
bamboo into shorter lengths
to get one length 11 inches
with a node at one end.

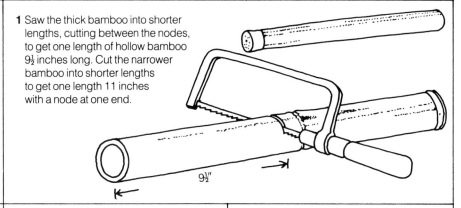

2 Cut a slit 4 inches from one end of the
thick bamboo with the penknife, always
pointing it away from you. Then carve
a rounded V shape back to join the slit.

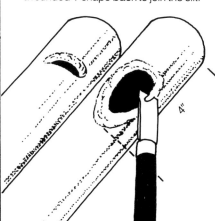

3 Shape the mouthpiece. Turn the
bamboo around, finding the center
of the back. Now starting $\frac{3}{4}$ inch
down from the top, carve off an
angled section of the bamboo.

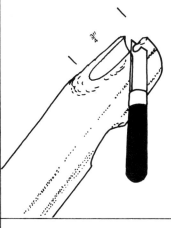

4 Take the cork and first sand it down
lengthwise and then sand it so that
the rounded side is beveled
1 inch down.

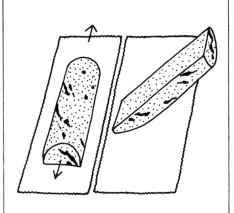

5 Push the cork firmly into the thick
bamboo until $\frac{1}{4}$ inch shows in the hole
on the front and it fits snugly into
the larger angled hole at the back.
Cut off any extra cork left at the top.

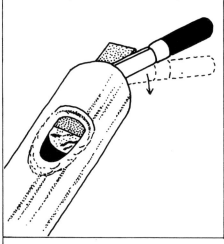

6 Sand the end and beveled edge of the
cork so that they are both smooth and
flush with the bamboo edges.

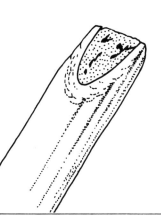

7 Carve a narrow groove $\frac{3}{4}$ inch down
from the top all around the open end of
the narrower bamboo. Wrap with cotton
balls, then a circle of rag, and
secure with thread tightly around the
groove.

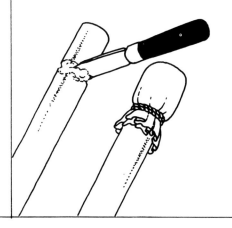

8 Blow the tune while simultaneously
pushing the stopper up and down.

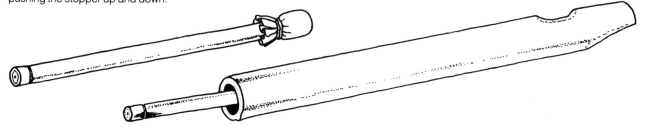

THE NATURAL SYSTEM OF COLOURS

the PRISM; *where we find the orange colour lies between the blue and red: which, thus regularly succeeding each other, gave the first hint, that they should be placed in a circular form* ... MOSES HARRIS 1766

In the fifteenth century Leonardo da Vinci, in his Treatise on Painting, while listing the colours in order of importance as being white, yellow, green, blue, red and black, made no attempt to assemble them in any other order.

In the seventeenth century Sir Isaac Newton devised a colour circle in order to illustrate that a beam of white light passed through a triangular prism would divide into a number of chromatic rays. He took the colours red, orange, yellow, green, blue, indigo, and violet, linking them into a circle.

During the eighteenth century two important works on colour were published. The first, a Treatise on Colour by the German engraver Jakob Christoph Le Blon, stated that all other colours could be derived from red, yellow and blue – such a simple observation seemed hardly possible, but speculation changed to admiration as his findings were quickly proved correct. The second, a slender book by an English entomologist, Moses Harris, was to become a rare and much sought after work. His earlier publication,

The Aurelian, a huge volume filled with detailed illustrations of butterflies and moths, each meticulously reproduced in their natural colourings, led to his interest in the subject of colour. The Natural System of Colours is barely ten pages long yet it provides a totally comprehensible account of the relationship of one colour towards another. The author explains how the first hint that colours could be linked naturally came to him when he noticed that orange came between blue and red as they came from the prism. He illustrates this point with two circles, the PRISMATIC, composed of colours derived from the three pure colours red, blue and yellow, and the COMPOUND composed of colours derived from the three muted colours, orange, green and purple.

Throughout the nineteenth and twentieth centuries a number of beautifully produced books were published explaining how one colour can be related to another, but of them all Moses Harris's short treatise remains the clearest.

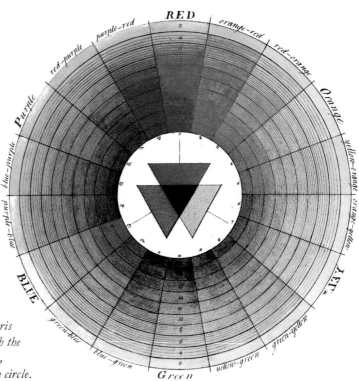

'The Prismatic Circle' *which Moses Harris devised to illustrate the simple way in which the three primitive colours red, yellow and blue, could be* **naturally** *linked together to form a circle.*

JENNY'S FIRST COLOR CIRCLE

You will need

2 18″ × 24″ sheets heavy watercolor
  paper
3 tubes of Winsor & Newton paint
  from their Cotman watercolor range:
  Cadmium Lemon
  Permanent Blue
  Alizarin Crimson
A good paintbrush
Drawing things including compass,
  protractor, ruler, pencil, and eraser
Paper scissors
White paste
A jam jar for water

NB Work over newspaper

Special notes

After painting each color or
combination of colors, wash the brush
and change the water.

1 On each sheet of paper make one large
circle with two smaller circles inside.
Set the compass first at 3½ inches, then
at 2⅜ inches, then at 1³⁄₁₆ inches, drawing
on each sheet of paper in turn. Place
the protractor over the center and
mark off every 60 degrees all the
way around. Rule across the
circles from mark to mark through
the center. This divides the circles
into six sections. Now erase every
other line within the second and
center circles as clearly shown in
step 3.

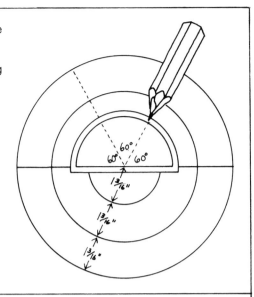

2 Write, very lightly in pencil, on each
section of both circles the color or
combination of colors shown on the
drawing. Cut out both circles, keeping
one whole and cutting the other into
the twelve sections.

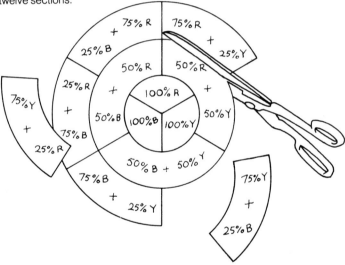

3 Paint the three small sections cut from
the center circle in red, blue, and yellow.
Once dry, put them in their place on the
uncut circle.

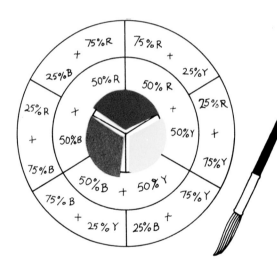

4 Paint the three sections of the second
circle, mixing the three basic colors as
instructed. Once dry, put them in their
place on the uncut circle.

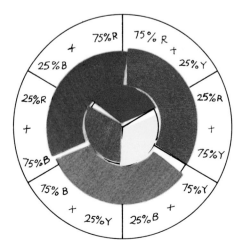

5 Complete the color circle by painting
the six remaining sections as instructed.
Once dry, put them in their correct place
on the uncut circle. Stick all the
sections down.

BOOMERANGS

'The young English boy must not expect to be able to make anything more than a plaything out of this interesting weapon, he can neither afford the time nor get the teaching necessary for the mastery of it.'

THE BOY'S MODERN PLAYMATE Circa 1899

To the Aboriginal people, who have occupied Australia for more than 40,000 years, the boomerang is a means of survival and so a necessity in their everyday life. The 'beaked boomerang' in the hands of a skilful thrower becomes a lethal war or hunting weapon. But its efficiency depends as much on the time spent in producing it as the skill in launching it. A carefully selected piece of shaped hardwood, two or three metres long with a naturally hooked end, was rubbed down and the inside edge sharpened. Next the wood soaked, dried and made pliable over an open fire. Finally symbols were scratched on the surface and filled with coloured pigments to convey the warrior's message – a language which has subsequently enabled historians to identify the different tribal areas. At a very early age Aboriginal children play with the 'cross spinner' – a toy made from woven pandanus leaves which, correctly guided, spins to the ground. Next they learn how to throw the boomerang, practising with a simple cross of wood secured with reeds. The technique once mastered, children graduate to a single curve of wood which, properly thrown, will encircle a planned distance and return to its starting point. Known as the 'returning boomerang' it is this which has become so much a part of the traditional games and current competitions of Australia. In 1981 an outward throw of 107m (351ft) was made by Bob Burwell and recorded in the Guiness book of Records as the longest outward throw ever made. The longest return throw recorded is 370m (1,127ft), an unofficial distance also recorded in 1981.

'Emu Hunt and Chase of the Chinese'
by Tommy McCrae – a pen and ink drawing made during the nineteenth century.

RORY'S RETURNING RULERANG

You will need

2 wooden rulers
Fine sandpaper
Small bradawl
Linen thread
Darning needle
A pair of gloves
and access to an open space.

1 Sand down each side of the top surface of both rulers. If the rulers are already beveled you will have less sandpapering to do, but you must sand off the sharp corners.

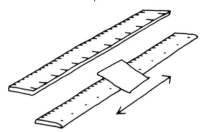

2 Make a hole exactly in the middle of each ruler with the bradawl.

3 Put the rulers, beveled side up, on top of each other at right angles. Stitch them firmly in this position with diagonal stitches, using the linen thread. Knot and cut off the end.

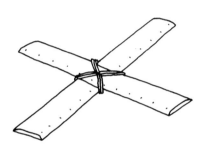

Take the boomerang and the gloves and hurry off to an open space.

4 Grasp the bottom of one ruler with the inside of your fingers on the flat side and your thumb up the edge nearest your body.

5 Face the wind, turn 45 degrees to the right, and put your left foot forward. Hold the boomerang at eye level and slightly behind your shoulder.

6 Swing your body first right, then left. Throw the boomerang with a flick out toward the right.

7 A lot of practice is necessary. If the boomerang lands in front of you, then it is being thrown too far to the right; if it lands on the left behind you, then you are throwing too far to the left. You may also need to change your position if the wind is strong or light. Experiment!

8 Once you have mastered the technique and think there is a chance of catching the returning boomerang —please wear gloves.

55

WOODEN JOINTED DOLLS

'I long to try my limbs a bit,   *Our joints are good*
And you must walk with me;   *Though made of wood,*   *And I pine for liberty.'*   BERTHE UPTON 1895

The earliest surviving wooden jointed doll, made during the first century A D, is thought to have been a companion for the grave rather than a plaything for the nursery. But whatever the object of its creation, it is an inspired piece of Roman craftsmanship. Carved in oak, the mortice and tenon joints enable the arms and legs to bend easily.

It was this versatile movement which led to the two successful careers of the wooden jointed doll. As nude models (or lay figures, as they were often called), they provided the artist with a realistic reminder of the movements and proportions of a human body, with the advantage that they could be ordered in any size. As mannequins (or fashion dolls, as they were commercially known), they were attired in the latest French fashions and

despatched on sales trips to the Royal households throughout Europe during the fourteenth century. Once the outfit had been ordered the dolls were passed to the little princesses and became much treasured possessions.

Because it was less fragile and more versatile than its competitors the wooden jointed doll was always a favourite. 'Dutch dolls', a name which they acquired as they travelled through Holland in the early nineteenth century, were made by German foresters who put the long winter months to productive use making simple wooden dolls. Masquerading under a variety of different names such as 'Wooden Bettys', 'Peg Dolls' and 'Pennywoods', the few that have survived are now beginning to find their way to the museums.

The earliest example of a wooden jointed doll, found in a Roman tomb of the first century A D.

A Cartload of Dolls, *one of the amusing illustrations done by Florence Upton for her sister's story, 'The Adventures of Two Dutch Dolls and a Golliwog', first published in 1895.*

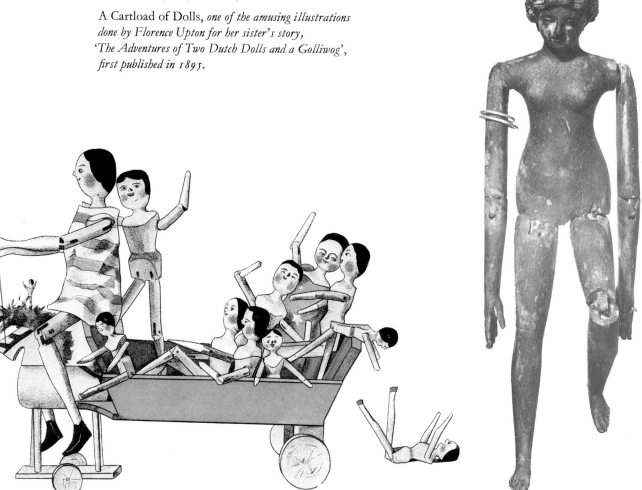

JOINTED JESSICA

You will need

One 2½″ wooden ball
6″ length of 1⅜″ wood dowel
3′ length of 3/16 × ¾″ wood
Four ½″ 3mm bolts and nuts
Four 1″ × 4 gauge round-
 head screws
Four ¾″ escutcheon pins
One 2″ × 8 gauge dowel
 screw
6 small ⅜″ wooden beads
Oil paints for hair, eyes, and mouth
Fine paintbrush and paint thinner
Length of material 16″ × 12″
A yard of bias binding
Scrap of felt for shoes
Some thread elastic
Sewing things and scissors
A soft pencil and a ruler
Carpentry tools including a
 medium and small bradawl, a
 hammer, plane, pliers, and small
 screwdriver. Work on a piece of old
 wood or a large pile of newspapers.

1 Prepare a hole ⅜ inch deep at the bottom of the wooden ball with the medium bradawl. Hold one end of the double-ended screw with the pliers and turn the wooden ball around and around onto the free end of the screw.

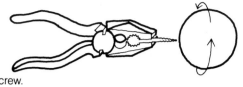

2 Prepare a hole ⅜ inch deep in the center of one end of the round dowel with the medium bradawl. Hammer the four wooden beads around the hole with escutcheon pins. Screw the ball firmly into the dowling until it rests neatly on top of the beads.

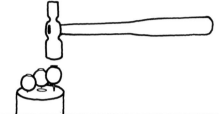

3 Cut the wood into eight lengths of 3 inches each with the fretsaw. Carefully round the ends with a plane which you use rather like a nail-file. Watch you don't scrape your knuckles! Smooth the edges with sandpaper.

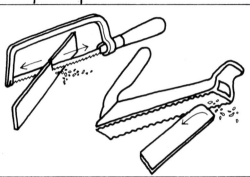

4 Take four of the cut lengths and mark them ⅜ inch in from each end. Mark the four remaining lengths ⅜ inch in from just one of the ends.

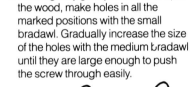

5 Working very gently so as not to split the wood, make holes in all the marked positions with the small bradawl. Gradually increase the size of the holes with the medium bradawl until they are large enough to push the screw through easily.

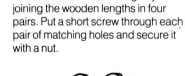

6 Make two arms and two legs by joining the wooden lengths in four pairs. Put a short screw through each pair of matching holes and secure it with a nut.

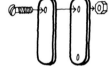

7 Measure and mark the round dowel on each side, ⅜ inch down for the arms, ¾ inch up for the legs. Prepare holes at the marks with the medium bradawl. With the nuts on the inside, first thread the limbs on the long screws, then the wooden beads. Screw the limbs firmly into the prepared holes.

8 Cut out a dress from the apron project (page 9) but instead of taking measurements, simply fold the material, lie the doll sideways on top, and cut out the apron shape around her.

9 Paint her hair and face and leave to dry while you get on with sewing the dress. Follow the apron project but forget about the elastic at the wrists. Run a short length of elastic thread around the neck to gather it in.

10 Once the doll is dry and dressed, cut out and stitch together some felt pieces to cover her cold wooden toes.

PAPER

RAGS *make paper,* PAPER *makes money,* MONEY *makes banks,* BANKS *make loans,* LOANS *make* *beggars,* BEGGARS *make* RAGS.   ANON. eighteenth century

The Chinese discovered how to make paper in the first century AD. They used to soak either mulberry bark, old fishing nets or fragments of silk in the river, then beat the material to pulp, spread the fibrous remains on a framework of thin bamboo strips and left it in the sun to dry. The craft remained a well kept secret until the eighth century when, during a battle in Central Asia, several Chinese papermakers were taken prisoner. Ordered to pursue their native work but unable to procure either mulberry bark or rags they substituted the local hemp and flax – so it was that the prisoners of Samarkand, in revealing their secret, were also responsible for the first major development in paper making.

In the twelfth century when the craft finally reached Europe, it was the Spanish who introduced a water-powered machine which mechanised the laborious process of making pulp. A century later the Italians produced 'watermarks', using them creatively as a private language between themselves, rather than commercially as the trademarks which they later became.

By the fifteenth century mills in France, Germany and the Netherlands were well established and paper was first produced in England. Up until the seventeenth century the English paper industry imported its materials, but a plague, thought to have been generated by packages of contaminated rags, obliged the government to find an alternative supplier. Some years later a law was passed forbidding either linen or cotton to be used in burying the dead – a practical piece of legislation which provided the paper industry with 200,000 pounds of extra material every year!

Although throughout the last few centuries machines have been developed to handle efficiently every stage of commercial paper production, the craft of handmade paper has changed little since its original conception; and the watermark, now considered a foolproof device against the forger, retains its original charm and creative possibilities.

A print from one of a series of wood blocks made by the Japanese artist Hokusai 1760–1849.
Three important stages in papermaking are evident – the man washing and softening the mulberry bark in the river, the woman beating the fibres to pulp – and in the background, sheets of paper seen drying in the sun.

You will need
A stencil alphabet of 1″ letters
2 baking dishes
Blue food coloring
Ruler
Masking tape
Red colored pencil
White wax crayon
A pad of white writing paper and
    matching envelopes
A tray and permission to use the iron
    Paper towels

1 Prepare the stencil. Cut the initial from the alphabet and put it on the bottom of the tray. Run a line of masking tape along the top and bottom, leaving 4 inches of tape on either side of the letter.
Then peel it up, turn it over, and seal the sticky side of the tape with another couple of strips of tape.

2 Position the stencil centrally at the top of the paper. Trim the ends of the tape straight with the edge of the paper on either side.

3 Stencil the outline only of the initial with the red colored pencil. Put the stencil to one side and rule a red line down either side of the paper about ¼ inch in from the edge.

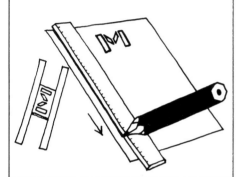

4 Fill in both the stenciled outline of the letter and the extreme margin at either side of the paper with the white wax crayon. Use the point to fill in the letter and the end to fill in the edges.

5 Fill one of the dishes with water and submerge the piece of paper. Fill the second dish with water and add a teaspoonful of blue food coloring. Stir. Transfer the sheet of paper from the clear to the colored water. Leave soaking while you work on the next sheet, getting it to the stage of clear water.

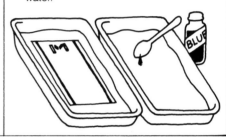

6 When the second sheet is ready to be submerged in the colored water, remove the first sheet and lay it face upward on the top of the tray. Put the tray upright over the sink to drain. Blot out any air bubbles and excess water with a mop of paper towels.

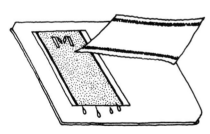

7 Transfer the second sheet from the clear to the colored water and start on a third sheet. While this is soaking in the clear water, take the first sheet from the bottom of the tray and hang it over a broomstick stretched between two chairs.

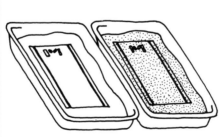

Transfer the second sheet to the tray —first draining, then mopping—and the third sheet to the colored water, and start on the fourth sheet. Repeat until you have completed the number of sheets required.

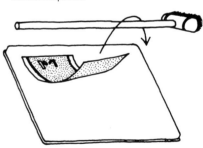

8 Once dry, iron the paper. Put it face down on a paper towel on the ironing board and simply iron the back. Remember to turn off the iron after the last sheet.

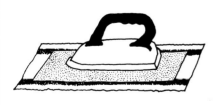

9 On the envelopes simply draw a line about ¼ inch in all around from the edge with the red pencil. Keep the colored pencil with the writing paper; if the letter is short and dull the matching pencil will cheer it up.

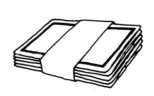

QUILLS

'*A serpents tooth bites not so ill,*
As dooth a schollers angrie quill'   JOHN FLORIO 1591

Local materials provided ancient civilisations with different writing implements; sharp stones were used to scratch symbols on limestone, sticks to mark tablets of clay and camel hair brushes to inscribe walls. Important business was recorded with a reed quill on a papyrus leaf, a combination which was used by the Italians during the Middle Ages and led to the development of the feather quill. They established an excellent system using a special reed stylus to score a wax coated surface. The surface could be recoated and so used over and over again. Not surprisingly this ingenious method continued to be used by both school children and students, even after the quill pen and paper had been declared by the scribes and scholars as the perfect combination.

By the fifteenth century pen-making was a recognised trade and quills were sold in the shops. A quill pen was made from a primary feather taken from the wing of a goose, crow or raven; this was trimmed, scraped and cleaned, the soft tip hardened in hot ashes, then shaped to a point and split. With the sale of each pen went advice for its maintenance and the owner was advised to keep the tip of the quill clean and submerged in water. Failure to do this resulted in a stiff and inflexible pen just like the reed tip which the quill had replaced. A good sharp knife was an essential accessory – not only to reshape the tip which wore down easily, but also to scratch out any mistakes which might be made. Despite the invention of the steel nib and its subsequent improvements, there are many calligraphers who still prefer to work with a quill.

A young Scholar,
painted by Jan van Scorel, 1531.

You will need

2 wing feathers of an English or
   Canadian goose!
2 ballpoints, a red and a blue
2 cans of model paint, in red and
   blue
A square-ended paintbrush, turpentine,
   all-purpose glue, and a lump of
   reusable sticky putty
Short piece of 13amp fuse wire
Sheet of fine sandpaper

1 Take the red pen to pieces by gently pulling the ballpoint and its ink-filled tube from the outer plastic case.

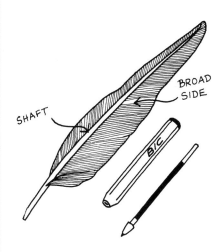

2 Snip off the end of the quill. Bend the wire in half and gently push it up and down and around the shaft of the quill.

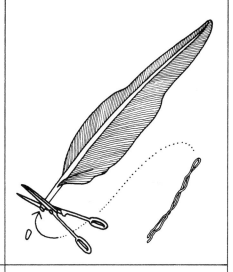

3 Push the ink tube gently into and up the shaft. When it will go no further, measure the amount still sticking out between the top of the metal ballpoint and the bottom of the quill. Withdraw the tube and cut the equivalent amount from the top of the tube. Seal it with the putty.

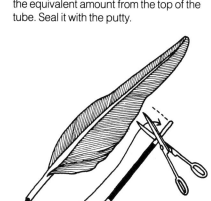

4 Push the ink tube back up the shaft again, making sure the neck of the ballpoint fits neatly into the end, then take it out.

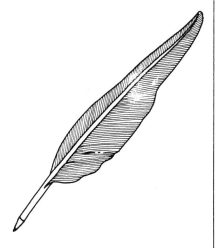

5 Cut the broad side of feathers away from the quill as close to the roots as possible.

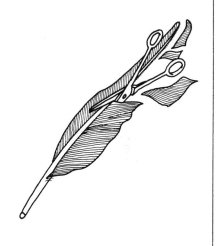

6 With sandpaper, remove the remaining whiskers; then rub down the quill as well, so as to make a surface suitable to paint.

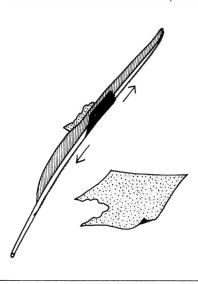

7 Push the wire gently back into the shaft. Use the end as a handle and paint the quill with red paint. Once painted, stick upright into a blob of putty. Complete the other quill in the same way, using the blue pen and the blue paint. Leave them to dry overnight.

8 Once dry, put a tiny circle of glue around the necks of the ballpoints and push them gently into position, making sure you have the red with the red and the blue with the blue!

PAINTED FINISHES

. . . there are few respectable houses erected, where the talent of the decorative painter is not called into action, in graining doors, shutters & wainscots, & etcetera. NATHANIEL WHITTOCK 1827

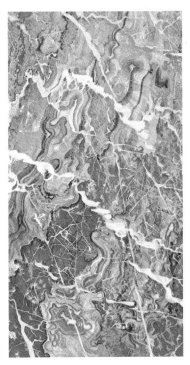

Four plates taken from the Van der Burg's book 'School of Painting for the Imitation of Woods and Marbles' published in 1878. The black and white engravings show the necessary tools for each skill. The coloured illustrations – the final stage in imitating wood and marble. The comments and colours are quoted from the book.

St Remi Marble – *derives its name from the place where it is found, St Remi, on the frontiers of the Grand-Duchy of Luxemburgh.*
The palette is white, jet black, yellow ochre, chrome-orange, Turkey red, colcothar and ultramarine blue.

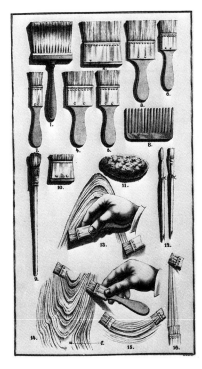

Trompe d'oeil is an elaborate form of decorative art whereby a flat surface is cunningly arranged to provide the illusion of a three dimensional object. The earliest example of trompe d'oeil is provided by a number of old fish bones depicted in a Roman mosaic pavement of the third century BC.

Mural painting was widespread in Italy during the fourteenth century and trompe d'oeil was an important aspect of the Renaissance painter's work, since the better his understanding of perspective and shadow the more convincing was his work. In the sixteenth century classical ruins became a popular theme, with columns realistically puddled or veined to depict the true characteristics of marble.

Marbling and graining, although often created to provide a handsome finish, rather than realistic imitation, still lurk under the shadow of trompe d'oeil. Both became important aspects of interior decoration throughout Europe during the seventeenth century, when wooden columns and fireplaces were elaborately marbled, doors and wainscoating exotically grained.

In the eighteenth century paint was used to create a lighter and more romantic effect. Stippling was introduced, a fine coat of colour worked over a white background until the white became vaguely visible, resulting in a much gentler surface than flat paint.

In the nineteenth century books explaining and illustrating the colours, tools and techniques of experts like Nathaniel Whittock and the Van der Burgs were readily available and showed a trained house painter how to extend his skills to marbling, graining and stippling. In the twentieth century, J. P. Parry, wrote two similar but simpler books, now sadly out of print, which enabled even the amateur to create an interesting decorative system by ragging or stippling a wall, or to transform the surface of a dreary piece of wood into an exciting painted finish.

Walnut – *belongs to the most esteemed species of wood used by joiners and imitated by painters.*

The palette – ivory black, Cassel's Earth, Burnt Sienna, and a little Prussian blue.

FROM PLASTIC TO POTTERY POTS

You will need

Two 4″ and two 3″
   plastic flowerpots and saucers
4 suitable houseplants
Clear polyurethane
Model gouache paint in white,
   olive green, and brown
2 square-ended paintbrushes
1 mop-headed paintbrush
A small piece of rag
Paint thinner
Distilled malt vinegar

1 Turn the flowerpots upside down over your hand and give them a coat of white paint with a square-ended brush. Really work the paint into the surface. Paint the outside of the saucers. Leave to dry overnight.

2 Paint the inner rims of the flowerpots and the insides of the saucers with the white paint. Leave to dry overnight.

Repeat steps 1 and 2 so that everything gets two coats of white paint.

3 Take two pots, one of each size, and their matching saucers. Squeeze out a length of olive-green gouache paint on the saucer, moisten with vinegar to the consistency of light cream. Cover the white painted surfaces with the mixture, using the second square-ended brush.

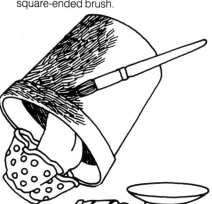

4 Take the mop-headed brush and bounce it over the wet surface. This process is called stippling. Stipple one set of pots and matching saucers. Leave to dry overnight.

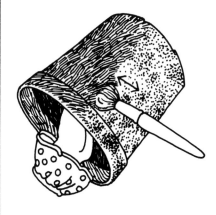

5 Cover the second set with the mixture of brown gouache and vinegar. Then taking the small piece of rag, arrange it in random folds and lightly blot it over the wet surface. This process is called ragging. Rag the second set of pots and saucers. Leave to dry overnight.

6 Apply a coat of polyurethane over all the painted areas and leave to dry overnight.

Once dry, plant the pots. If they are for a yard sale remember to charge handsomely for the very special pots.

PATCHWORK

Life is like a patchwork quilt　　*Some patches are rosy, happy and bright,*
And each little patch is a day,　　*And some are dark and gray.*　ELIZABETH DECOURSEY RYAN

Patchwork, like most cottage industries, originated from necessity. Carefully saved scraps of woollen materials, cut into strips and squares, were stitched at random to each other to provide warm coverlets for everyday use.

The earliest English example of a patchwork quilt, made at the beginning of the eighteenth century, was inspired by a topiary garden. Different shaped patches cut from a variety of imported Indian cottons were appliquéd to the background then quilted. By the middle of the century an abundance of imported materials had led to a more sophisticated form of patchwork; a simple shape, repeated in different cottons, butted and stitched together, over and over again, resulted in a large geometric pattern.

This basic principle provides the foundation to American patchwork, which from the onset has a very much more sociable and imaginative history. Nearly always a community project, each quilt was made from a number of individually worked 'blocks', each block consisting of four or five different shaped patches, repeatedly joined together. Based on the graphic images of everyday life. 'Goose Tracks', 'Broken Dishes', 'Spider's Web' and 'Lone Star' are only four of over a hundred traditional designs. The 'Bridal Wreath' was a particular favourite, scraps were quietly exchanged, patches secretly stitched into blocks, a 'quilting party' arranged at which the blocks were sewn together, the engagement announced and everyone thoroughly enjoyed themselves.

Meanwhile the craze for patchwork in England during the nineteenth century saw the production of printed central panels and matching borders – stitching time was halved and patchwork quilts were even prettier. Sadly, no short cuts were available to the English soldier whose occupational therapy was to stitch patches, nor to the country schoolgirl, often tearfully obliged to complete her daily quota of patchwork.

 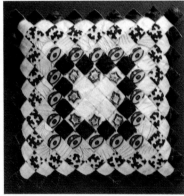

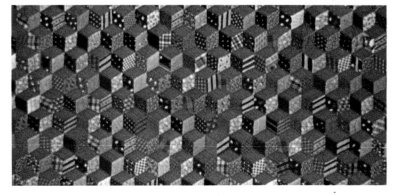

Private Thomas Walker painted by T. W. Wood, convalescing in a military hospital in 1856.

The facsimile of an English Victorian patchwork cushion. Each side has 145 patches.

A detail from an American mid-nineteenth century quilt.

A REVERSIBLE PATCHWORK CUSHION

Materials required

A 12″ × 12″ cushion pad
* 10″ in one colored gingham
  10″ in a second color of
  the same gingham
¼″ square graph paper, ruler, pencil,
  scissors, and sewing things
* one colored gingham is both described
  and depicted throughout
  the illustrations as 'spotted' in order
  to avoid any confusion!

1 From each material you need thirteen square and four oblong patches. On squared paper, rule off twenty-six blocks of 12 × 12 squares and eight blocks of 12 × 36 squares. Cut them out. These are the templates.

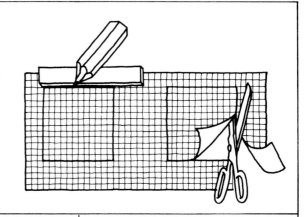

2 Pin half the templates on each material, allowing an extra sewing margin of ¼ inch around each. Square the templates with the printed lines on the gingham and cut out the patches.

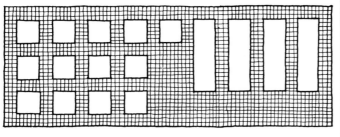

3 Tack the material around each template, keeping the sides very straight and the corners neat and square.

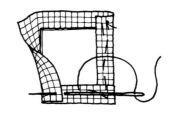

4 Join the patches. Face together a gingham and a spotted patch. Neatly sew them together along the top of the squares. Open the two squares and join a second spotted patch down the left-hand side. Open the three squares and join a third spotted patch along the bottom. Open the four squares and join a fourth spotted patch up the right-hand side.

5 Sew a gingham patch in each corner.

6 Sew a spotted oblong patch on each side.

7 Complete the block by stitching a gingham patch in each corner.

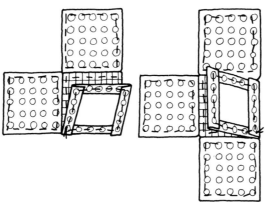
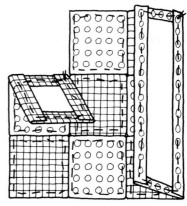

8 Using the completed block as a guide but reversing the color ways, complete a second block of patchwork.

10 Stuff the cushion pad into the gap and stitch up the two oblong patches.

9 With the two completed blocks facing each other, sew them together, leaving an opening the length of an oblong patch along one side. Remove all tacking and carefully keep the templates for re-use.

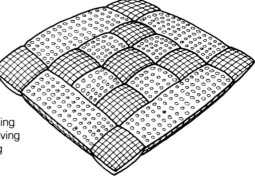

CRACKERS

'An evening party supper without Tom Smith's crackers would be like a banquet without a dessert!'

THE AMERICAN REGISTER 1900

The cover of a Tom Smith catalogue in 1902, one of the possible choices then available. Each box contained a dozen crackers, each cracker a novelty relating to the subject on the box, a hat, a motto and of course a banger.

A holiday in France, during the early part of the nineteenth century, led to the invention of the cracker. Tom Smith, an English confectioner, taken by the French style of wrapping sweets, returned to England to copy the idea. The same sweets, originally sold loose in paper bags, rolled in twists of brightly coloured paper sold twice as fast. He then developed the idea by including an inner wrapper on which a motto was printed, another successful notion which boosted the sales figures and led him to believe firmly that anything enterprisingly wrapped would be a guaranteed success. Not so, his next venture, packaging toys in a similar manner, was a dismal failure. A setback which he may well have been thinking about when a new idea was triggered in his mind.

The story goes that standing by the fireside one Christmas, Tom Smith, deep in thought, became suddenly bemused by the merriment which might be caused if a paper log, filled with surprises, were to crack and spark as it opened. The surprises were at hand, the wrappings simple, for he had merely to draw on previous experience. But the bang proved a considerable challenge with endless necessary experiments before the 'snap' was both safely and effectively mastered.

His ingenious idea was an immediate success and, while retaining his interest in the confectionery business, Tom Smith opened the first cracker factory in 1847. By the turn of the twentieth century a considerable variety of crackers, often referred to as 'cosaques' or 'bon-bons', packed in boxes of a dozen, suited to every occasion and priced accordingly, were available. A similar situation still exists today with Tom Smith's firm as busy as ever – they maintain that if the thirty six million crackers they made last year, were placed end to end, they would stretch from their factory in Norwich to their novelty supplier in Hong Kong.

In a catalogue of 1888, the Crackers for Bachelors included a pawn ticket, hair dye and a shirt button while the box for Spinsters included a night cap, a thimble and a powder puff. In 1900 Crackers à la Française had love mottoes printed both in French and English while the box of Crackers for Boys illustrated 'Larks in a College Dormitory'. It seems the possibilities and permutations had no bounds.

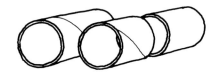

Materials required

Tiny presents
Homemade paper hats and
    handwritten jokes
* Cracker bangers
Crêpe paper
Metallic tape
Silver stars or leaves
Paper cake decorations or doilies
Shiny ribbon
Aluminum foil or metallic silver paper
Cardboard tubes 1½″ in diameter
Scissors, thin string, and a ruler

NB One cake decoration will only decorate
three crackers. The insides of toilet-paper
rolls provide excellent tubes!

Special note

* If the bangers you have bought seem too
short, add a bit of double-backed tape to
each end.

1 Cut one cardboard tube down to 4 inches
long and cut another in half. The two
shorter lengths may be used again and
again.

2 Cut a length of foil 6 inches × 10 inches
and a length of crêpe paper 6 inches ×
14 inches. Make sure that the grain runs
lengthwise.

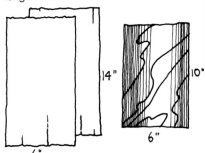

3 Roll the present and the joke up in the
paper hat and put the package into the
longest tube.

4 Place the shiny side of the aluminum foil
down on a flat surface. Center the crêpe
paper on top of the foil. Lie the banger
along the center. Put the filled tube over
the banger.

5 Take the short tubes and, putting an end
of the banger in each, lie them on the
paper, 1½ inches away from the central
tube.

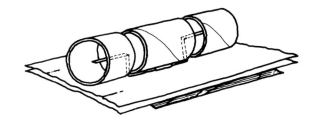

6 First check that everything is evenly
spaced and centered. Then roll up the
cracker, securing it with six bits of
metallic tape.

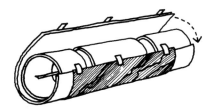

7 Tie lengths of string between the tubes
and very gently gather in the folds. When
tight, knot and cut off the ends. Push the
short tubes inward.

8 Cut a length of cake decoration 6 inches
long. Stick on two lengths of metallic
tape, leaving ¾ inch extra at each end to
secure the decoration around the barrel
of the cracker.

9 Cut a second strip of cake decoration 6
inches long. Cut again lengthwise to
provide two long elegant bands. Secure
these at each end of the cracker with a
strip of tape half stuck to the band and
half stuck to the cracker.

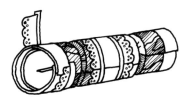

10 With shiny ribbon, make and secure the
main decoration, and fringe both ends
of the cracker.

Finally, take out the two short tubes and
keep them for the next cracker.

STENCILLING

'The diaper covering the whole of the cella walls is identical . . . showing stencilled rows of seated Buddhas, dark brown borders, etc.' SIR MARC AUREL STEIN 1921

Paper patterns, pierced with holes marked by red earth, provide evidence of the earliest stencils. Dating back to the tenth century AD these were used to repeat the outline, over and over again, of the figures which line the caves of a Thousand Buddhas in Western China.

It was not long before people realised that if they made the holes larger a complete image could be successfully reproduced. Costumes were elaborately decorated in this manner and stencilling became a recognised trade of the East with its competitive techniques passed secretly down from generation to generation.

Stencilling was not extensively employed in Europe until the fifteenth century when it was used mostly to compliment other crafts; it enabled craftsmen to repeat a decorative border or simple design quickly and was itself an effective form of decoration. It provided an accurate method of overlaying colour on to an otherwise black and white design – playing cards and later wallpapers were originally coloured in this manner. Indeed 'flock' wallpaper was actually created by stencilling the design in paste directly on to the paper which was then sprinkled with powdered wool.

Stencilling became very popular in America because imported wallpapers, however simple, were so expensive. Even at the turn of the nineteenth century, when wallpapers were more easily and cheaply available, the travelling painter still managed to lead a carefree life, stencilling the home in exchange for board and lodging.

ABOVE: *This preaching Buddha was traced from the pricked outlines of a similar stencil. It was painted on paper then stuck on a wall. Although the size of each Buddha was exactly the same, the painters always introduced variety by using three or four simple colours, arranging them alternately in each row of figures on the wall, so that they made a pattern.*

BELOW: *This stencil was one of many stencils actually used during the tenth century* AD *to make identical images of the Buddha on the walls and ceilings of the cave temples at Dunhuang, in far west China, where it was a part of the discovery by Sir Marc Aurel Stein at the beginning of the twentieth century.*

You will need
A stencil alphabet
Roll of masking tape
Paint
Varnish
Paintbrushes and cleaner
Household sponge
Newspaper
Saucer
Scissors and reusable sticky putty
Tape-measure
Ruler and T-square

Special notes
Letters may be duplicated by tracing, then transferring the outline to watercolor paper, cutting the holes, then sealing with two coats of clear varnish.

1 Cut the alphabet. Cut centrally between the letters, re-trimming any excess paper so that the letters will lie totally flat beside each other.

2 Line up the letters on a working surface, using a ruler and set square to make sure they are straight.

3 Run a line of masking tape across the top and then across the bottom of the name.

4 Fill the spaces between the letters with narrow strips of masking tape.

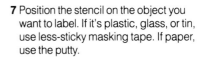

5 Pull the ends of the masking tape off the surface, and gently turn the assembled name over.

6 Put fresh masking tape over the sticky side of all the tape on the back of the stencil. It is now ready to use.

7 Position the stencil on the object you want to label. If it's plastic, glass, or tin, use less-sticky masking tape. If paper, use the putty.

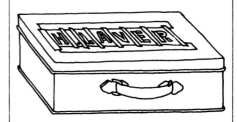

8 Squeeze some paint out on the saucer. Tear off a small cube of sponge and wet it, then squeeze out as much moisture as you can. Work it around in the paint until it is evenly absorbed, then bounce it over newspaper a few times to get rid of the excess moisture.

9 Use one hand to bounce the paint through the openings of the stencil and the other to keep the individual letters flat to the surface. Leave to dry.

10 Carefully remove the stencil and wipe it clean. Dry between sheets of newspaper under a heavy book before re-using. If necessary, varnish over the stenciled name.

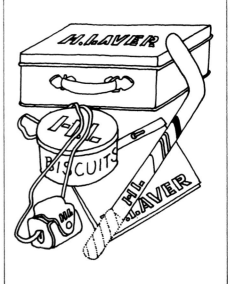

KAI-AWASE

Those who play well appear to be concerned only with the shells arranged before them, but they are really keeping an eye on the sleeves and knees of their opponents. YOSHIDA KANEKO Essays in Idleness 1330

ABOVE: *Women playing the shell game. One of a series of illustrations made by the Japanese artist Utamaro for a book printed in the eighteenth century.*

CENTRE: *A closer look at some of the shells.*

BELOW: *Lacquer boxes and shells from a game made during the seventeenth century.*

Among the great wealth of treasures assembled by the Royal Academy for their Japanese Exhibition in 1981–82 was 'a set of equipment for the shell game'. This consisted of two tall cylindrical boxes and a number of clam shells. Face down the shells looked much like any other shells, but face up they were simply enchanting – tiny scenes painted in bright colours and embellished with gold illustrated different aspects of everyday life in Japan during the seventeenth century.

Kai-Awase, as this particular game is called, originated in the twelfth century from a children's game of matching shells in pairs – a feat in itself for only the natural pair will match exactly. For this more sophisticated game one hundred and eighty pairs of shells were required. Each pair had a theme, and each shell was decorated with an aspect of that theme. Originally the players were required simply to match the illustrations, but as time went by Kai-Awase became far more complicated than just a fashionable parlour game.

In one variation a good classical education was a distinct advantage for, in picking up one shell, on which perhaps the ending of a poem might be inscribed, the player was obliged to recite the beginning of that poem before being allowed to pick up a second shell. In another variation a sound general knowledge was a great asset for, if a player picked one shell on which some particular subject was painted, being able to elaborate on the theme of the illustration secured extra points.

Young brides-to-be were greatly encouraged to play as it was thought to broaden their minds and make them aesthetically aware of their surroundings. Indeed, no dowry was considered complete without a set of Kai-Awase. The shells, freshly decorated and still hinged in their natural pairs, were neatly packed into two beautiful lacquer boxes and on the eve of the wedding some mutual friend could carry the game to the bridegroom's house. A heavy responsibility, for, should the shells become separated on the journey this provided a bad omen for the marriage which might also become separated. On the other hand, if they arrived intact, then the couple were destined to live happily ever after.

SATSUKI'S SHELL GAME

You will need
* 15 attached pairs of cockle shells
  A bottle of clear nail varnish
  A dessertspoonful of chlorine bleach
  A packet of self-adhesive numbered
  labels
  Paper towels and a dish
  Sharp, pointed scissors

* a couple of extra pairs are useful.
  Mussel shells can also be used.

Rules
Much like the game of concentration, the object of the game is to collect as many pairs as you can. As the backs of shells are more recognizably matched than the backs of cards, only one extra turn is allowed after making a pair.

1 Keep the shells in attached pairs. Gently clean them and leave to soak in a dish of water with a spoonful of chlorine bleach.

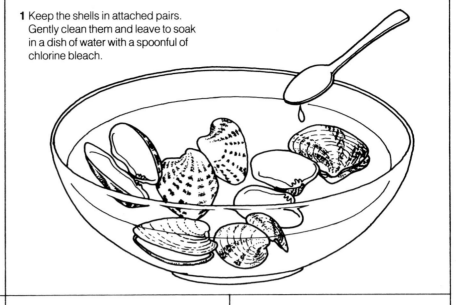

2 Take a pair of shells and gently dry them with a paper towel. Take two sheets of matching numbers and stick no. 1 on the inside of each shell. Number all the pairs of shells, each pair with a matching number.

3 Separate the shells. Use sharp scissors rather than your fingers as the tough membrane tends to break off pieces of shell.

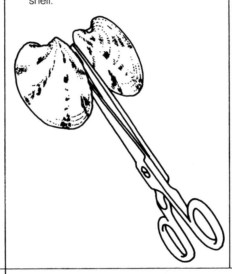

4 Varnish all the insides of the shells. This seals in the number and strengthens the shell. Leave to dry.

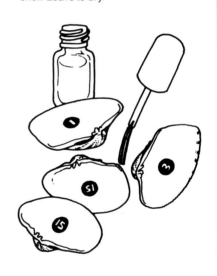

5 Varnish all the outsides of the shells. This shines the surface and again strengthens the shell. Leave to dry.

6 Arrange the shells in a series of four circles. Put 1 in the middle, then surround it with 5, then with 9 and put 15 around the outside. The game is now ready to play.

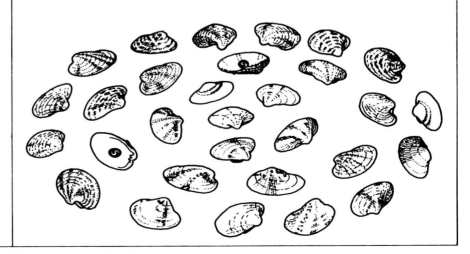

MAKEUP

'In England the young, old, handsome, ugly, all are bepatch'd till they are bed-rid. I have often counted fifteen patches, or more, upon the swarthy wrinkled phiz of an old hag three-score and ten upwards.'   FRANCIS MISSON 1698

Mr Grimaldi. in his favorite Dance of "Fun and Physic". in the pantomime of "The Rival Genii." as performed at Sadlers Wells. in 1814: Drawn by T. M Grimshaw. who performed with Grimaldi. at Covent Garden and Sadlers Wells Theatres in 1814.15.19.20.21.22.23.

By 10,000 BC painting the body was part of the daily routine of Egyptian life. Natural minerals such as iron oxide, malachite, lead and copper ores were used, pounded to powder then softened with saliva. Eyes were heavily blacked, veins over-painted in blue, nipples coated in gold and the oil from a castor plant considered an adequate cleanser. However, by the fourth century AD the Queen of Bavaria, whose skin lotion was said to be brewed from boars' brains, crocodile glands and wolves' blood felt that the fresh warm milk of a donkey provided a more effective method of cleaning the skin.

By the sixteenth century physicians had come to deplore the use of make-up; and the church, for quite different reasons, proclaimed it to be the invention of the Devil. But whether used to ward off evil spirits, protect from the sun or attract their fellow beings, fashionable women were put off neither by the threat to their skins nor by the threat to their souls. Seventeenth century faces were caked with make-up and littered with patches – tiny symbols in black silk, cunningly positioned to indicate the wearer's political views or romantic inclinations.

By the eighteenth century lead based creams had been recognised as the cause of rotting teeth, wrinkles and baldness; one skin lotion, containing mostly arsenic, claimed over five hundred victims before its inventor was arrested and executed!

In the nineteenth century fashionable make-up became taboo, while stage make-up took on a new dimension; actors and acresses would create their own theatrical image often with the most disastrous effect. The twentieth century recognises the contribution of 'make-up artists' whose work is greatly respected by their fellow technicians and whose talents are as much appreciated by the confident film actor as they are by the nervous television guest.

Joseph Grimaldi *on stage in a pantomime at Sadler's Wells in 1814. The watercolour drawing was done by T. K. Grimshaw, who for many years performed with Grimaldi at Covent Garden and Sadler's Wells.*

You will need
20 colorful pieces of cotton strips,
  2″ wide × 10″ long
20″ of ribbon
A Ping—Pong ball
Some narrow adhesive tape
Red elastic thread
A plain white swimming cape
Scarlet enamel paint
Scarlet lip liner
Black eyebrow pencil
Cake of white eyeshadow
Small sponge and saucer of water
Paintbrush and turpentine to clean it
Needle, scissors, and soap

NB It all washes off in the bath!

1 Cut a piece out of the Ping-Pong ball, try it on, and re-cut to fit snugly over the nose and allow normal breathing. Pierce holes on each side. Paint and leave to dry.

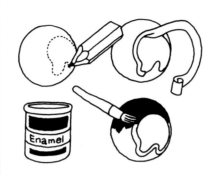

2 Wet your finger, rub it around and around in the soap, then smooth your eyebrows down firmly.

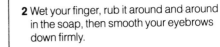

3 Put on the cap to keep your hair out of the way and make your face look bigger. Rub the damp sponge over the white eyeshadow and gently smooth it all over your face. Pat on a second layer.

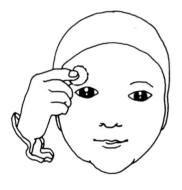

4 Draw a triangle on either side of your chin with the black pencil. Then draw a pair of new eyebrows 1 or 1½ inches higher than your old ones and a set of eyelashes ½ inch lower than your own.

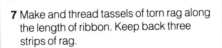

5 Use the red pencil. Draw a new bottom lip curving into a huge smile; fill in your own top lip. Draw and fill in two interestingly shaped cheeks and two triangles on the cap.

6 Knot a length of looped elastic to each side of your new red nose. Fit the loops over your ears under the cap.

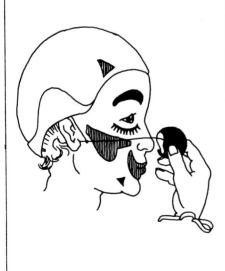

7 Make and thread tassels of torn rag along the length of ribbon. Keep back three strips of rag.

8 Knot and tape the three remaining strips of rag at the sides and on the top of the cap.

KITES

Grand and majestic soars my paper kite,
Through trackless skies it takes its lofty flight:
Nor lark nor eagle flies to such a noble height.   ADELAIDE O'KEEFFE Circa 1800

There are many conflicting legends regarding the origin of the kite but most historians are agreed that kites existed in China by the third century BC. Whether the Chinese used them to measure the distance between one army and the next, to carry rope across an otherwise impassable river, or simply to alarm the enemy with the illusion of falling stars, their warriors considered these earliest kites vital in warfare.

Nowadays in China and Japan kites have their own battles, and while on such occasions the sky is silently filled with a competitive mass of brightly decorated birds and fish, there is noisy agitation below among the fliers and gamblers whose fortunes may well depend on how skilfully they guide their paper creatures.

Kites were introduced into Europe during the fifteenth century, where they remained nothing more than an amusing game until the eighteenth and nineteenth centuries. It was during these years that the unique advantages of the kite in advancing science and technology came to be fully recognised. Benjamin Franklin used a kite with a key attached to its string to demonstrate to a small boy how, in a thunderstorm, lightning running down the wet string caused sparks to fly from the key. Sir George Cayley incorporated a kite in his design for the first model glider and Lawrence Hargrave invented the biplane box kite. This last invention led Captain Baden Powell, younger brother of the founder of the Boy Scout movement, to devise an air lift using a train of kites to raise a man off the ground. This achievement in turn led the Wright brothers to experiment with the production of gliders which finally resulted in their first successful aeroplane flight.

ABOVE: Tametome, *the warrior, when imprisoned on an island, attempted to reach the mainland by means of a giant kite.*

Kite fliers painted during the nineteenth century by the Japanese artist Kunisada.

You will need

29″ of either fine lawn cotton or finest polyester lining and corresponding thread

6½ yds of ribbon 1½″ wide

Two 17¾″ × ¼″ dowels

A shuttle of kite string

A large-format newspaper

A ruler, pencil, scissors, and pinking shears.

1 Cut a folded sheet of newspaper so that it is 18 inches long and 11 inches wide. Make a mark 4⅜ inches from the top and rule across. Along the top, the ruled line and the bottom, mark 5⅛ inches and 6 inches. Join the marks from the top to the bottom. Rule a diagonal line from the 6-inch mark at the top to the edge of the drawn line. Draw another diagonal line from this point to the 6-inch mark at the bottom. Cut out along these two diagonal lines. This is the paper pattern.

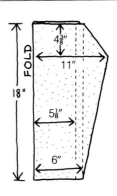

2 Lie the folded material on a flat surface, with the selvage edge at the top and the folds on the left side. Pin the paper pattern directly on the top—the folds on the left and top exactly over the selvage of the material. Cut out with pinking shears.

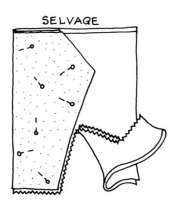

3 Unpin the paper pattern, keep it folded, and cut off the right-hand side of the 6-inch line. Open up the material and pin the unfolded paper pattern back onto it. Use a line of tacking stitches through the material to mark up either side of the pattern.

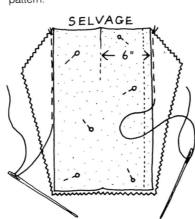

4 Unpin the pattern, refold and cut off the outside strip at the 5⅛-inch line. Repin onto the material and again mark up the sides with a large tacking stitch.

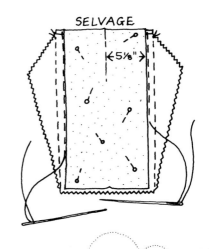

5 Fold between the tacking lines. Retack along the line and secure with a small running stitch.

6 With the pinking shears, cut two 1½-inch lengths of ribbon, pin, and stitch over the pointed corners. Make a hole right through the center of each patch and buttonhole-stitch around it.

7 Slide the dowels into the pockets.

8 Stitch ¾ inch of ribbon over the top of each pocket to seal in the dowling. Halve the remaining ribbon and stitch firmly to secure the other ends of the pocket, leaving the tails trailing.

9 Cut a length of kite string 4 yards long. Thread through the holes on the points and knot. Make another knot 1½ inches from the central loop.

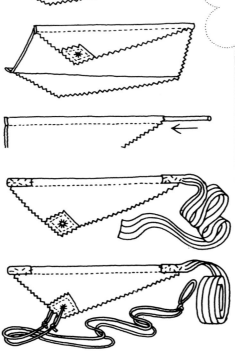

10 Thread and knot the kite line through this last loop and hurry to a windy spot!

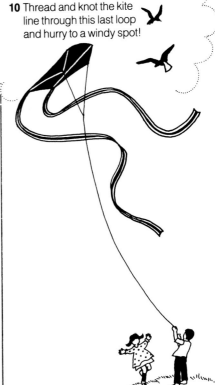

THAUMATROPES

'The inventor confidently anticipates the favour and patronage of an enlightened and liberal public on the well-grounded assurance that "one good turn deserves another".' JOHN AYRTON PARIS 1825

Having qualified as both a doctor and inventor at the beginning of the nineteenth century, Dr Paris's first practice was in Cornwall. There he devised a gadget to cut out the danger of premature blasting in the tin mines, which made working conditions much safer for many of his patients. He moved to London and by writing medical books and articles won the respect of his colleagues and earned enough extra money to provide his only child, Thomas, with a sound education.

To encourage Thomas and his schoolfriends with their lessons, Doctor Paris wrote a little book aptly entitled 'Philisophy in Sport made Science in Earnest' – a mixture of fact and fiction in which the main characters are a boy called Tom, home from boarding school for the first time, his sisters Laura, Fanny and Rosa, their father Mr. Seymour and his friends, the Reverend Twaddleton and Major Snapwell. They are all there to encourage Tom to continue his studies throughout the holidays. His sisters ask relevant questions, the learned vicar makes profound observations, and the hearty major takes a keen interest as Mr. Seymour's abundant knowledge and ingenious inventions demonstrate to Tom the laws of gravitation, geometrical definition and atmospheric vibrations. Mr. Seymour goes on to explain the persistence of vision, how one image made on the retina of the eye is retained for long enough for a second image to be superimposed upon the first; to illustrate his explanation he made an amusing toy – a round card with the drawing of a cage on one side, a rat on the other and with strings at either side. 'This is termed a Thaumatrope,' he announced. A word which the vicar immediately explained to the children was of Greek origin, 'Exactly, a wonder-turner,' agreed Mr. Seymour, who proceeded to whirl the card as he asked 'Why is this rat like an opposition member in the House of Commons, who joins the ministry?' His audience watched fascinated as the rat became visually trapped in the cage, 'Ha, Ha, Ha,' retorted the major, as he read the answer, 'because by turning round he gains a snug birth, but ceases to be free.' More riddles and thaumatropes were produced and, whether or not the children understood the jokes, the merriment of the grown-ups must have provided a happy atmosphere to an unusual lesson. Sadly, the book does not relate whether or not Tom came first in class on his return to school.

A Cruikshank drawing illustrating Dr Paris' book.

An early thaumatrope and original box.

A LOVING THAUMATROPE

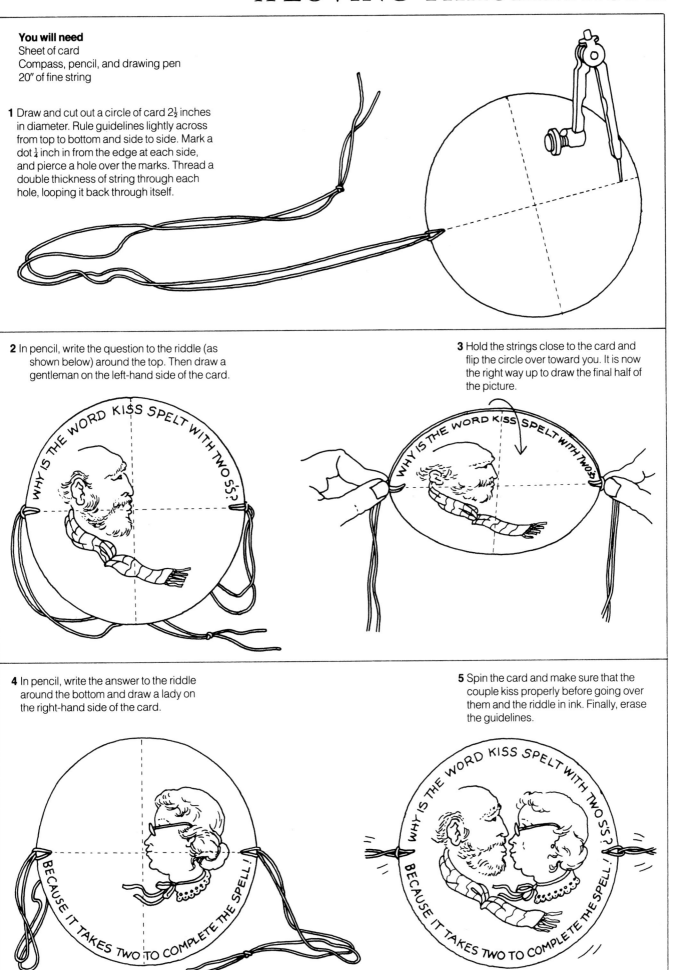

You will need
Sheet of card
Compass, pencil, and drawing pen
20″ of fine string

1 Draw and cut out a circle of card 2½ inches in diameter. Rule guidelines lightly across from top to bottom and side to side. Mark a dot ¼ inch in from the edge at each side, and pierce a hole over the marks. Thread a double thickness of string through each hole, looping it back through itself.

2 In pencil, write the question to the riddle (as shown below) around the top. Then draw a gentleman on the left-hand side of the card.

3 Hold the strings close to the card and flip the circle over toward you. It is now the right way up to draw the final half of the picture.

4 In pencil, write the answer to the riddle around the bottom and draw a lady on the right-hand side of the card.

5 Spin the card and make sure that the couple kiss properly before going over them and the riddle in ink. Finally, erase the guidelines.

ORIENTAL LACQUER

'no damp air, no mouldring worm, or corroding time, can possibly deface it.' STALKER AND PARKER 1688

Lacquer was first employed by the Chinese over 2,000 years ago when they discovered the natural juice of the tree, Rhus Vernifera, provided the basis of an effective coating. Its efficiency as a preservative is demonstrated by the survival, in perfect condition, of a huge pot, moulded in hemp and paste and coated with lacquer, made during the early part of the third century BC.

Although decorative lacquer work is thought to have been introduced into Japan during the fourth century AD, it was the rapid spread of Buddhism during the sixth century which saw the turning point in its history. Temples and shrines shot up everywhere, Buddhas were moulded in every shape and size, and the art of Japanese lacquering flourished.

Just as the Rhus Vernifera, whose sap provides the basis of lacquer, is indigenous to the East, so is the skill in its application. The tree sap once cleaned, purified and dehydrated is kept airtight at a controlled temperature until required. The surface to be lacquered – bamboo or wood, moulded paper or hemp – is meticulously prepared and only when a porcelain smooth finish is achieved can the laborious task of the 'layerist' begin. Each layer of lacquer, once applied, has to dry and

harden before it is ground down and another layer applied; the necessary number of layers is dictated by the final decorative effect required. *Makie*, a technique employed by the Japanese since the tenth century, where the decoration is sprinkled in powdered metals between the layers of lacquer would, on a flat object, only require a base of ten layers. Whereas for carved lacquer, the finest specimens of which were produced by the Chinese Imperial factories during the seventeenth century, it was considered necessary to apply at least fifty layers, laid in different colours, before the lacquer could be carved effectively!

Travellers returning to Europe in the seventeenth century, while united in their admiration of lacquer, were unable to believe it could have been done by even the most skilled of craftsmen. They debated its origins – was it the complicated notion of a genius or merely the simple invention of the devil?

At the beginning of the eighteenth century the French led the field in producing an imitation of lacquer, but neither this nor any subsequent shiny finishes which masquerade under the name should be confused with genuine oriental lacquer.

A box of different coloured layers of lacquer carved with peaches, characters and flowering sprays. Chinese 1522–1566.

An Inro of gold and lacquer in the form of a box. Japanese, second half of the nineteenth century.

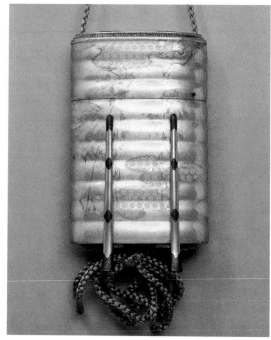

LACQUERED FOR LILY

You will need
An interestingly shaped cardboard
  box
Scarlet and black gloss paint
Clear polyurethane
Winsor & Newton ink in nut brown and
  deep red
2 square-ended brushes marked
  black and red
1 mop-headed brush
1 varnish brush, $\frac{1}{2}''$ size
A small natural sponge
Sheet of waterproof sandpaper
Paper towels
A couple of cans to support box while
  it dries and old newspapers to work
  over

Special notes
Wash any brushes you use for the
paint or polyurethane immediately in paint
thinner, and those that you use for ink in
water.

1 Neatly paint the inside of both the lid and
bottom of the box with black paint, using
the appropriate square-ended brush.
Leave to dry overnight, paint again the
following day, again leaving it to dry
overnight.

2 Paint the outside of both the lid and
bottom of the box with red paint, using
the appropriate square-ended brush.
Leave to dry overnight, paint again the
following day, again leaving it to dry
overnight.

3 Take two small pieces of sandpaper and
rub them around and around against
each other until they feel hardly abrasive
at all. Saturate with water and gently
smooth the red painted surface with a
circular movement. Wipe dry.

4 Dip the mop-headed brush into the dark
red ink and cover the top and sides of the
lid. As the ink starts to separate, paint
over it again. When it starts to become
tacky, bounce the sponge over the inked
surface.
Repeat the process on the bottom of the
box. Leave to dry overnight.

5 Using the varnish brush, cover the top,
bottom, and sides of the lid with
polyurethane. Apply with long, light, even
strokes, once only. Repeat on the top,
bottom, and sides of the box. Leave to
dry overnight.

6 Repeat step 3.

7 Repeat step 4, but this time use the nut
  brown ink.

8 Repeat step 5.

9 Repeat step 3, remembering that the
  sandpaper should hardly be abrasive at
  all or it will scratch and spoil your work.

10 Apply one last coat of polyurethane and
  leave to dry for two days before
  assembling the lacquered box.

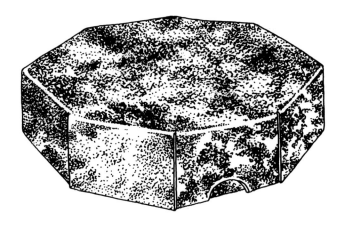

RATTLES

Tweedledum and Tweedledee
Agreed to have a battle;
For Tweedledum said Tweedledee
Had spoiled his nice new rattle. LEWIS CARROLL

An early function of the rattle was to frighten the devil and shoo away his demons. But of course there were other uses, for the charming clay pig, the earliest known example of a rattle, would have been incapable of such a task. The bronze rattles which survived the eruption of Vesuvius three hundred years later, however, provide good examples of the type of rattle used in such rituals.

Hathor, the mythical goddess and mistress of music, is often depicted with a rattle in her hand. Her worshippers sincerely believed in its mysterious powers over evil and the rattle's magical association, like its role in music, varies in importance from country to country. Its role as a child's plaything remains constant throughout the world, with rattles ranging from a simple gourd filled with dried seeds to the silvergilt heirloom dangling with bells.

During the Middle Ages bells were blessed and exorcised so that in summoning the congregation to church they dispelled any unwelcome spirits lurking in the air. Coral, shaped naturally as a wolf's tooth, was hung round a baby's neck in the belief that its symbolic form would keep evil at bay, and in the sure knowledge that its hard insoluble surface would provide a comforting teething stick. Miniature bells and coral sticks, mounted together in silver or silvergilt, elaborately engraved and often incorporating a whistle, became the recognised features of the craftsman's rattle. A child's plaything? Hardly, for no sooner was the christening over than this fascinating 'toy' was locked away and something not nearly so pretty produced in its place.

An Egyptian sistrum or ritual rattle – similar to those which survived the eruption of Vesuvius.

The earliest example of a rattle, Greek Hellenistic, dates from the 2nd century BC.

Carved and painted bird rattle from Haida in North America, where it was probably made in about 1840.

LEFT: *A rattle from Panama – the gourd is secured with a strip of leather to a naturally shaped bone handle.*

CENTRE: *A bronze pear-shaped rattle 500 BC, an archaeological discovery found in Ireland.*

RIGHT: *An English family rattle kindly lent by Miss Lily Ford, aged 3. It belonged to her maternal great grandmother.*

You will need

* * 3 large mesh hair rollers
* Three 8" squares of material
* Three 8" squares of lining
* Some crochet yarn
* A bell
* Small wooden beads
* Dried haricot beans
* Pencil and paper
* Sewing things including a tape measure and scissors
* * if necessary remove bristles

Special notes

It's fun to make the rattles different colors so that the baby can easily recognize its favorite sound.

1 Measure the length and circumference of a roller and make a paper template to wrap around it. Trace around each end and cut out the two circles.

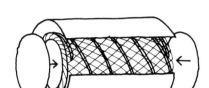

2 Pin the templates onto the fabric and, allowing an extra ⅜ inch sewing margin all around, cut out the shapes. Repin the fabric shapes onto the lining material and cut them out.

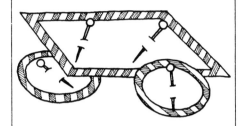

3 With fabric right-side up, lining underneath, put the two circles of material on the top of the roller. Turn down the edges, stitching them firmly onto the mesh.

4 Put in the bell and sew the remaining circle over the other end in the same way.

5 With the fabric right-side down, lie the lining on top. Fold and tack in ⅜ inch on each of the long sides and one of the ends.

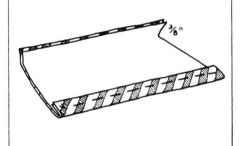

6 Roll the materials around the roller, using pins to secure them on either end. Turn in the end and pin down the overlapping materials.

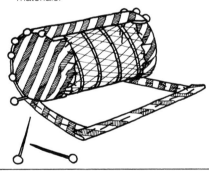

7 Replace the pins with tacking stitches around the ends and down the join.

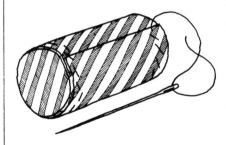

8 Using blanket stitch, sew firmly and safely together with the crochet yarn.

9 Cover the other two rollers in the same way, putting wooden beads in one and dried beans in the other.

10 Remove all the tacking and make doubly sure that you have not left any pins behind.

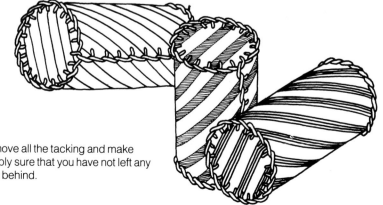

MINIATURE SHOPS

'Butcher Stores with papier mâché meat . . . $4.00, $4.25, $6.00.'   SCHWARTZ' CHRISTMAS BROCHURE 1910

A discovery in the tomb of Meket Re, an Egyptian official buried in about 2000 BC, provided the earliest example of a miniature market place. Complete with provisions and slaves, it represented the dead man's likely needs in the afterworld. Throughout the ages similar models must have existed as children's toys, but not surprisingly, none have survived.

Exquisite miniature shops and dolls' houses were produced in Nuremberg during the eighteenth century, assembled by the very same craftsmen and workshops that furnished the great castles of Germany. Perhaps they remain intact because they were commissioned by grown-ups as a curiosity for the drawing room rather than as a novelty for the nursery. So children must have been delighted when, at the end of the century, the toy manufacturer, Bestelmeier, produced an illustrated catalogue from which they could choose either a shop or a house and a selection of suitable furnishings to go inside them.

By the middle of the nineteenth century girls were being encouraged to learn cookery with a miniature kitchen that came complete with a recipe book, while boys were taught their basic sums on the scales and with the stock in a miniature shop. English butchers used miniature replicas of their shop, complete with sides of beef and potted geraniums, for Sunday's window dressing. By the end of the century toy manufacturers had extended their range to include shops of every variety – the most popular were the grocers and the post office.

This miniature butcher's shop, the ground floor of a Victorian dolls house, made in 1840, was probably designed as a child's toy rather than as a shop window display.

NUTTY'S FRUIT & VEGETABLE STAND

You will need

A plain white shoe box
Package of colored pipe cleaners
Paintbrush and paints
20 or 30 headless matches
Modeling dough (see page 27)
A piece of wallpaper 6″ × 11″
A button 1″ in diameter
Glue, ruler, and scissors
Beads, scraps of material, and sewing
    things

1 Make shoes for dolls, vases for flowers, pots for plants, fruit and vegetables with modeling dough. Make crates for the fruit and vegetables from cut lengths of matchsticks glued in layers.

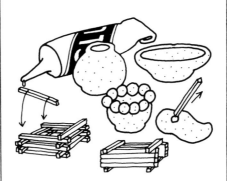

2 Line the bottom and sides of the shoe box with wallpaper. Turn it on its side. Rule off and color the bottom to resemble floor tiles. Measure the width of the lid into three equal parts. Cut off one third lengthwise.

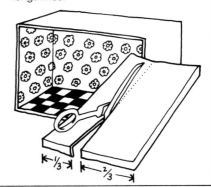

3 Take the narrower section. Find the middle of the cut edge and put the button centrally over it—allowing enough room to draw around the bottom. Make a row of half-circles in each direction. Cut out the scalloped edge.

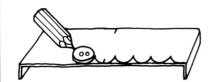

4 Measure 2¾ inches from each edge along the rim. Cut through the rim and bend up the central panel. Now glue the lid onto the box, leaving the panel sticking up.

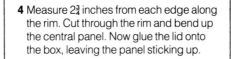

5 Take the larger section of the lid. Measure 4½ inches from each end along the cut and rim edges. Cut out the center panel. Measure the ends of the lid, divide in half, cut through the rim only.

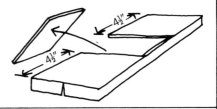

6 With the inside of the lid uppermost, rule across from one cut to the other. Score over the line with closed scissors. Bend in the sections.

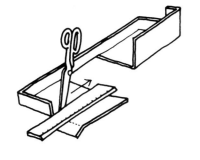

7 Glue the section in position, with the long rim under the bottom of the box and the two adjoining rims up the sides. Push the bent-over top inside the rims, gluing to the inside of the box to make counters.

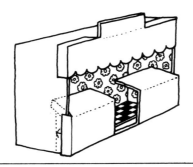

8 Paint the shop. Write the signs in pencil first, then paint and leave to dry.

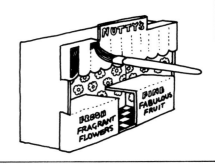

9 Thread a pipe cleaner through the wooden bead. Secure hair on top of the head with the short length. Twist more lengths around the first to add arms and legs to the body. Paint the face. Once dry, make and stitch on some clothes and stick the feet into the modeled clogs.

10 Make plants and flowers with pipe cleaners, put them in the pots and vases, the fruit and vegetables in the crates, and fill the shop.

FLORA DELANICA

'. . . the only imitations of nature I have ever seen from which I would venture to describe botanically any plant without the least fear of committing an error.' JOSEPH BANKS

Portrait of Mrs Delany painted by John Opie in 1782.

Born in 1700, Mrs. Delany had a happy childhood until, at seventeen, she was 'married off' to a rich old squire. He drank a lot and suffered from gout – a blessing in disguise as, confined to his bedside, she took up needlework and in respites, studied nature.

Widowed at twenty-four, she enjoyed a fashionable social life. She loved drawing and embroidery, reproducing flowers skilfully from a realistic rather than artistic point of view. While holidaying in Ireland she met a Dr. Delany whose company she apparently enjoyed a lot. The protestant clergyman must also have privately cherished their meeting, for when his wife died, ten years later, after a respectful two year gap, he wrote, proposed and married her. She was forty-two, he fifty-eight.

Dr. Delany stimulated her talents – the walls of his parish church were covered with shells, the kneelers most beautifully embroidered. His parishioners, too, were constantly encouraged by her enthusiasm.

Happily married for twenty-five years, it was a sad Mrs. Delany who, on the death of her husband returned from Ireland to live in England. An old friend, also widowed but with a large house in the country, suggested they spent some months each year together. As they shared friends and thrived on a common interest in botany it was an ideal arrangement. From the constant flow of visitors the most grand were the king and queen, George III and his wife Queen Charlotte, but the most appreciated were the botanists, Joseph Banks and Philip Miller.

Mrs. Delany was seventy-four when one day she spotted the similarity of some red paper to the colour of a geranium and quickly snipped out a few petals. That was it – the birth of a new pastime. More of a career perhaps, for over the next ten years, Mrs. Delany cut nine hundred and eighty 'paper mosaiks', all minutely correct, labelled both in Latin and English, each an exact replica of a botanical specimen, made up from hundreds of tiny pieces of coloured paper. A collection she affectionately nicknamed 'Flora Delanica'.

The 'Blush Rose' and the 'nodding thistle' – just two of the 980 'paper mosiacks' cut by Mrs Delany.

BELLA'S FLOWER COLLAGE

You will need
A dandelion
Layout pad, pencil and eraser
Square-ended paintbrush
Olive green, chrome yellow, and
  raw umber watercolor paints
White plate or palette
Good pointed scissors and tweezers
Piece of card 10″ × 8″

Special note
It is difficult to show in black and white a subject that depends a lot on subtle color for its finished effect. But press on, it's much prettier and easier than it looks.

1 Study the dandelion, its leaves, petals, and stem, and its different shades of color. Draw a simple pencil outline of the dandelion on the sheet of card.

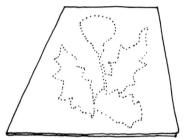

2 Take the layout pad and color two sheets of paper for each of the four color combinations you will need, as follows:

i. Paint the basic size and shape of the flower three times with four or five brushstrokes in yellow. Make additional single brushstrokes on a second sheet of paper in varying lengths and depths of color.

ii. Paint the basic shape and size of the leaves in green, making additional single brushstrokes on a second sheet of paper.

iii. Squeeze out a blob of yellow and a blob of brown paint side by side on the palette. Drag the brush between them so it is half yellow and half brown. Cover a sheet of paper in brushstrokes. Repeat on a second sheet, allowing the colors to merge.

iv. Use green and brown paint in the same way on the last two sheets.

3 Build up your flower on the card. First cut out, overlap, and paste down the three basic yellow shapes over the outline. Cut out the additional petals from the different-toned brushstrokes; arrange them realistically, pasting as you go along.

4 Cut the stamens from the brown strokes, making them nice and skinny. Put them in position, one on top of the other. This is a delicate operation, and tweezers are better than fingers.

5 Complete the flower with a layer or two of petals in front of the stamens, remembering that if you vary the tones your flower will look more realistic.

6 Build up the leaves, covering the outline with the green basic shapes first. Leaves curl over and the shading is difficult to copy, so use all the colors to get the right effect.

7 Paste down the stem and make veins on the leaves by pasting on the thinnest possible strips of the darkest color.

8 Make a separate label with the name in Latin and English, and paste it under the flower.

FOLDING FANS

'Women are armed with fans as men with swords, and sometimes do more execution with them'

THE SPECTATOR 1711

The accidental death of a bat during the seventh century AD is said to have resulted in the invention of the folding fan. The Japanese fan maker who witnessed the sad scene observed the formation of the bird's wing and, copying the mechanism precisely, adapted the principle to a sheet of paper. The development of skills and techniques with materials such as bamboo, sandalwood, tortoiseshell and ivory can be seen throughout the history of the eastern fan.

Although fans were in existence in Europe during the days of the Roman Empire, little was heard of them until the sixteenth century when, with a flourish, they were produced first in Spain then, via Portugal and Italy, arrived in France where fan making, which started as a pastime, went on to become a craft of major importance.

By the end of the eighteenth century the great artists of the day were painting fans.

There were fans specially designed for the opera, which included an optical lens for better viewing, quizzing fans, whose discreet holes gave the shy the confidence to look, fortune-telling fans, commemorative fans and mourning fans. And while the magazine, *Spectator*, published a witty article suggesting that the art of 'fluttering' the fan could be mastered in three months, the fan makers, Duvelleroy, invented 'The language of the Fan' – a series of risky gestures where the misplacement of a little finger on the guard converted an intended 'Hello' into a disastrous 'Goodbye'.

Sadly, the nineteenth century seemed to have little interest in the fan which, apart from a short revival towards the end of the last century and again in the twenties, seems almost to have vanished, but for its traditional role in the national dances of Spain.

A mask fan, *painted on vellum with ivory sticks, made in England during the eighteenth century, for the Spanish market.*

A FANFUL OF ICE CREAM

You will need
Good heavy watercolor paper
Unsmudgy colored pencils
Pencil, eraser, and scissors
Flat paintbrush
Small can of clear polyurethane
Paint thinner to clean brush
2 tiny two-holed buttons
Sharp needle
Sewing thread
Glue and Scotch tape

1 Draw a cone of ice cream, making sure that it drips over the left-hand side. Put a mark in the center of the bottom of the cone.

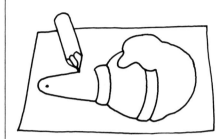

2 Trace the cone and retrace it onto a sheet of watercolor paper, making sure that the drip is on the left-hand side. Make nine more cones in this way, retracing from the original whenever necessary. Cut them out.

3 Color eight of the cones, filling them with different flavors. Leave the ninth uncolored and color the tenth with the drip on the right-hand side.

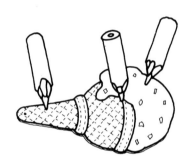

4 Lie them down on a sheet of clean paper and give them a coat of varnish. Once dry, turn them over and varnish the other side. Leave to dry.

5 Line up the cones with all drips on the left. Put the plain one second in the stack and the one you colored with the drip on the right at the end. Thread them onto the needle through the central marks.

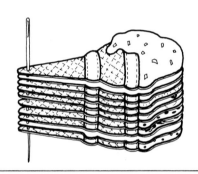

6 Put a button over the hole at the front and another at the back. Stitch them firmly, taking the thread right through the cones each time.

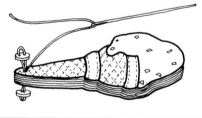

7 Start on the second cone. Secure the thread end with tape and stitch vertically backward and forward through the center of the rim of the third cone.

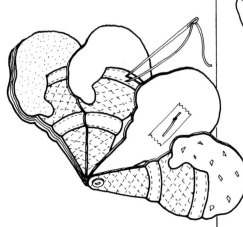

8 Gently pull up the thread so that the third cone is half masked by the second. Join the other cones in the same way, leaving the last one loose.

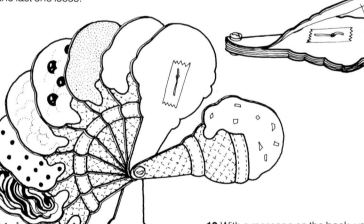

9 Hide the thread ends and tape by sticking together the first two cones and the last two.

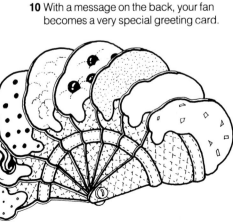

10 With a message on the back, your fan becomes a very special greeting card.

JEWELLED EGGS

'Eggs at 30,000 roubles . . .' AGATHON FABERGE

The Coronation Egg *contains the jewelled coach shown below. Every detail from the Imperial crown to the folding steps of the carriage is meticulously reproduced.*

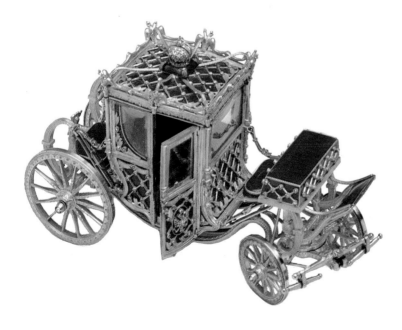

At last we can begin with 'Once upon a time there was a princess . . .' for indeed it was a princess who inspired her faithful prince to commission a most ingenious and extraordinary jewelled egg.

In 1884 Emperor Alexander III of Russia privately commissioned the young jeweller, Peter Carl Fabergé, to produce the first Imperial Easter egg. All were sworn to secrecy and even the Emperor himself was kept in suspense. This first Fabergé egg was not jewelled in the same intricate and glittering manner of his later ones, although perhaps it was best suited to the occasion of Easter. Nevertheless the workmanship was that of a genius. To all appearances it was a simple hen's egg. In reality the shell was gold, enamelled and polished to give the effect of an opaque white eggshell. The egg opened to reveal a textured gold yolk and within the yolk sat a chicken made from different golds, with engraved feathers and ruby eyes. The chicken opened and inside was a replica of the Imperial Crown within which lay a tiny ruby pendant.

The Emperor and his Empress were enchanted. Fabergé was granted the Royal Warrant and was given a standing order to produce a jewelled egg each Easter. Each egg was to be a surprise, but the Emperor was not above trying to get an inkling of what lay in store. To all the Emperor's gentle enquiries, however, Fabergé's respectful reply would be, 'Your Majesty will be well content.'

The tradition was established and on the death of Alexander III, his son, Emperor Nicholas II, increased the order to two eggs. One for his wife, the young Empress, and one for his mother, the Dowager Empress, who had originally inspired their creation.

Materials required
Piece of closely woven
   material 1' square
Box of pins
Beads and sequins
* A small bag of sawdust
Sheet of paper
Pencil and compass
Needle, thread, and scissors

* Sawdust is available from most pet
stores

1 Make the templates: Set the compass
with the point 4¾ inches away from the
pencil tip, and draw a circle on the sheet
of paper. Reposition the point anywhere
on the circle, and draw an arc through
the circle. Reposition the compass point
where the arc cuts the circle, continue
until you have a drawing like this. The six
boat-shaped sections are called
templates. Cut them out carefully.

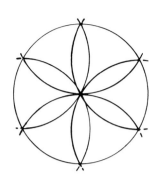

2 Pin the templates onto the material and,
allowing an extra ¼ inch sewing margin all
around, cut out the shapes.

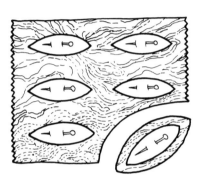

3 Tack the material around the templates,
making sure that the turning comes
exactly at the edge of the template.

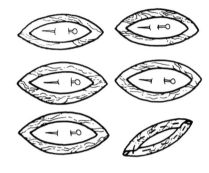

4 With the template side of the shapes
facing you, use small, neat stitches to
oversew the sections to each other.
When you come to the last section, finish
the stitches off ¾ inch before the end on
each side, leaving an opening.

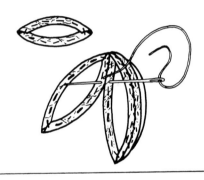

5 Remove tacking and paper templates.

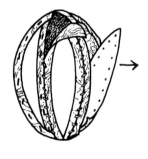

6 Turn the egg the right way out.

7 Stuff the egg with sawdust, packing it in
tightly.

8 Stitch up the gap.

9 Think about the decoration carefully so
that you do not run out of anything before
you have completed your egg!

10 Using a pin, pick up a tiny glass bead
and then a sequin, and push the pin
over the seamline into the egg. Cover all
the seams before adding any further
decoration.

Notes on projects

APPLIQUE *page 37*
Colored pipe cleaners can be bought in large art shops and specialist tobacco shops. Felt and burlap are obtainable from good craft shops; felt squares are the most sensible way of buying felt. We stippled the frame to match the strongest color in the picture. Instructions for painted finishes can be found on page 63.

APRONS *page 7*
Make sure all the materials are colorfast. One of the prettiest aprons we made was in plain cotton with the neck and hem bound in one color, the sleeves and pocket in a second, and the wrists in a third.

BOOMERANGS *page 55*
Impatience will spoil everything. If the corners of your boomerang are not safely sanded, someone else will end up in tears; if you're not prepared to practice, the project will be a disappointment.

BOWTIES *page 31*
White spots on a navy cotton background resulted in an elegant bowtie, while red silk moiré was a huge success.

COLOR CIRCLES *page 53*
We are grateful to Winsor & Newton, who suggested the mixtures. We chose their inexpensive London watercolor range for the project, but if you would rather use Artists' Water Colors then use Permanent Rose, Winsor Yellow, and Winsor Blue. If you prefer Designers Gouache, then use Rose Tyrien, Lemon Yellow, and Cerulean Blue.

CRACKERS *page 67*
Bangers may be ordered through Williams Sonoma, a nationwide chain of cookery stores. You can reach them at (415) 652-1515 to order bangers through the mail or to find the store closest to you. Although bangers are available in the stores only at Christmas time, they can be mail-ordered year-round.

EASTER EGGS *page 89*
A more practical but not quite so pretty present can be made by simply covering the seams with russian braid and filling in the panels with a pattern of color-headed pins.

FLORA DELANICA *page 85*
We chose a dandelion from sheer laziness – it was nearest the door on a rainy afternoon. Of course, any flower can be copied in the same way.

FOLDING FANS *page 87*
Made in card instead of paper, with flavors in two languages instead of greetings in one, this becomes a practical holiday accessory. For instance, if you are off to Italy, you write the flavor on the back of each cone, first in English then in Italian. Remember to put the words 'please' and 'thank you' on the first cone.

GINGERBREAD *page 13*
Mama Collins's recipe makes three dozen gingerbread men, so if you are just cooking for the family use a quarter of the ingredients. Gingerbread keeps well in an airtight tin, and a gingerbread man, with tinsel around his neck, stuck with egg white to a plain white card, provides an amusing Christmas card.

HOOKED RUGS *page 25*
To make a full-scale rug it is necessary to use either sacking or upholstery burlap – both have a much more open weave.

KAI-AWASE *page 71*
The shells are fragile and must be kept in a box. A household matchbox is the ideal size. We lacquered our box to match the color of the numbers used to pair the shells and lined the inside with felt. Instructions for lacquering can be found on page 79.

KITES *page 75*
The kite specialists Ambrose and Nicolette Lloyd kindly came to our rescue on this project. They suggested it, tested it, amended it, and gave it their seal of approval. The result, with the ribbons dancing in the sky, is very rewarding.

KNITTING *page 21*
If you knit a bead in the wrong place and only discover it a row or two later, don't panic and unhappily unpick it – carefully push the bead along the wool, in and out around the neighboring stitch until it is in the right position.

KNUCKLEBONES *page 27*
For a more colorful game use four fine colored pens to pick out each of the four patterns. Use the four faces to determine the score.

LACQUER *page 79*
It is imperative to use the materials we have listed. Be sure to rub the whole area of the sandpapers down, as one abrasive edge can ruin the lacquer surface, and take no shortcuts on the specified drying times. The result will then be stunning.

LINO CUTS *page 23*
We tried to be too clever by printing on to a gold shiny card – that was two years ago and the ink is still tacky!

MAKE-UP *page 73*
Stick to the method and materials which we have used. Lipstick smudges and then looks dreadful. The Ping-Pong ball smells horrid when first cut, but the smell will wear off.

MARBLED PAPERS *page 9*
Once you have mastered the art with one color, try it with two. Always experiment on a saucer of size first, as some colors are totally incompatible, some react strangely toward each other, and some are very beautiful.

MINIATURE SHOPS *page 83*
Shoe boxes appear to vary enormously in size – so measure your box carefully and adapt the project to suit its size. If you are impatient for the modeling dough to dry, then, on this occasion, as it doesn't matter if everything becomes a little rounded, put the things you have made on a baking sheet in a warm oven for half an hour.

MONEY BOXES *page 15*
The same project, with four or five white beans inside and two totally sealed ends, makes a successful large rattle for a crawler to pursue across the floor.

MOSAICS *page 19*
Any geometric design worked over the same number of squares and set within the same sized frame makes an attractive flowerpot stand.

PAINTED FINISHES *page 63*
The surface must be prepared with either an eggshell or flat oil paint, and this must be allowed to dry hard. Fluff-free sponges, rubber combs, and blobs of molded plasticine all provide interesting effects. If you don't like what you have done, simply wash it off – providing of course that you haven't put on a final coat of polyurethane.

PAPER *page 59*
This is a sad tale – we had hoped to be able actually to make paper – but after several experiments decided the result was not worth all the mess. It is a craft which requires either caustic soda or the use of a good mixer; being frightened of ruining ourselves with one and a much needed gadget with the other, we watermarked instead.

PAPIER MÂCHÉ *page 17*
Covering the mold with vaseline does make it easier to separate, but isn't strictly necessary.

PATCHWORK *page 65*
Using just the square patches, only 225 are required to make a crib cover large enough to tuck in at the sides. Lined with terylene wadding, quilted along the joins and backed with cotton, the crib cover makes a very special present for a new baby.

POMANDERS *page 11*
This was one of our earliest projects; the cloves are not in 'regimental' order nor does the ribbon fit neatly round the orange, but the pomander, made eight years ago, still smells delicious.

PORTABLE GARDENS *page 29*
Ours is nearly a year old. The soil is covered with a fine layer of moss and the plants are a marvelous bright green. We are a bit lazy about turning it around but do leave the cork off – for a couple of hours about once a month – when the plants get trimmed.

QUILLS *page 61*
It is not strictly necessary to trim off the broad side of the feather – in the old days both would have been trimmed – we thought the compromise was rather smart.

QUILTING *page 45*
Anything larger than a glasses or needle case should really be worked on a frame. Otherwise it tends to pull to one side, and you won't notice until the work is almost completed.

RATTLES *page 81*
If you only plan to make one, then stitch some ribbon around its middle, making the ends into a loop so that it can be tied to the side of the baby's basket.

REMEMBRANCE POPPIES *page 47*
With white crêpe paper instead of red, and pink instead of black, four sets of petals instead of two, shaped to curl inwards and not outwards, the project can be easily adapted from poppies to peonies.

SHELLS IN DECORATION *page 39*
This is also a marvelous means of disguising a well-made empty box, but do remember to plan it first on paper.

SILHOUETTES *page 35*
You can buy black-and-white film at drug stores. The paper most suited to the project is called black matt surface paper and is ideal as the tracing can both be transferred to and cut out on the white side. Art supply stores stock it.

SLIDE WHISTLES *page 51*
Providing that the bamboo is dry, the mouthpiece correctly shaped, the cork neatly fitted, and the mop head snugly blocking any escape of air, the whistle will play a complete scale.

SOLITAIRE *page 49*
The board must be left weighted on the bottom of the tray to dry – first top, then bottom – otherwise it will not be totally flat. We have an interesting example of a curly solitaire board!

STENCILING *page 69*
Cutting your own stencils, you must be very precise. It's hard work and necessary to use an extremely sharp knife, so consequently is rather dangerous – if you decide to try, there are a number of excellent books easily available on the subject.

STRAW MARQUETRY *page 41*
We completed the project, illustrations and all, before discovering that double-sided tape, carefully handled, provides the ideal solution. Cut the length of tape to the width of the paper in the direction the ribbon is to run. Stick it down. Peel back the protected paper. Cover the sticky surface with strips of ribbon. A little practice on a spare piece of graph paper might be a good idea.

THAUMATROPES *page 77*
Simply trace Anna's and spin it. Once you understand the principle, make your own caricatures of your friends with appropriate jokes – it will be a welcome change from the conventional greeting card and can be individually designed to suit every occasion.

VALENTINES *page 43*
This requires serious concentration. The project can easily be adapted to different shapes by simply drawing half of the final shape on the template which you make in step 7. It was inspired by a Christmas decoration made in Hong Kong.

WHIRLIGIGS *page 33*
It is essential to use a hole-punch to make the holes and pliers to bend the skewer. Unless the holes are clean and the skewer straight, the whirligig will not whirl.

WOODEN JOINTED DOLLS *page 57*
If you get the materials from a large do-it-yourself shop they will probably cut all the pieces to size for you and simply charge to the nearest convenient measurement. We used extra-long screws for safety's sake.

note Goop, a handcleanser obtainable from hardware stores, is an invaluable asset when working with oil paints or glue.

Acknowledgements and bibliography

It has been said that the writer who steals from one author is a plagiarist but the writer who steals from many is a researcher. As a researcher it would take me as many pages again to acknowledge fully all the books which I have consulted while compiling the historical sketches for Copycats. Sadly many of these are now out of print. In choosing books to recommend I have limited myself to the three books on each subject which I found to be the most informative, and I would like to thank all the staff in the libraries of the Victoria & Albert Museum, The British Museum and The American Library for their help during the course of my researches.

APPLIQUE *page 36*

The appliquéd hanging of the Tristram legend from the Victoria & Albert Museum.
Photography V & A Crown Copyright.
selected reading Encyclopaedia of Needlework – Thérèse de Dillmont 1907. Seventeenth Century Interior Decoration in England, France & Holland – Peter Thornton 1978 and chapters on Textiles by Donald King in the series of The Connoisseur Period Guides.

APRONS *page 6*

Pottery snake goddess from the Heracleion Museum, Crete.
Photography Ministry of Culture & Sciences, Athens.
The Dairywoman from the Museum of Rural Life, Reading.
Photography Institute of Agricultural History at the University of Reading.
selected reading Costume of Household Servants & Occupational Costume in England – Phillis Cunnington & Catherine Lucas 1967. The Book of Costume – Millia Davenport 1948. Modesty in Dress – James Laver 1969.

BOOMERANGS *page 54*

Tommy McRae's drawing comes from the collection of the National Museum of Victoria in Melbourne.
selected reading Boomerangs, Aerodynamics & Motion – Felix Hess 1975 (too vast and learned a book for the non-professional) and Aboriginal Weapons or Australian Boomerangs two leaflets readily available in Australia, but which barely touch on their history. Most of the information was gathered from the description cards in the South Australian Museum in Adelaide and the Museum of Mankind in London.

BOWTIES *page 30*

Delafontaine's painting is from the Musée de la Monnaie, Paris.
Photography Flammarion. Frontispiece of Neckclothitania from the book in the library of the Victoria & Albert Museum.
Photography Marianne Ford.
selected reading Histoire du Costume – Francois Boucher 1965. Fashion – Mila Contini 1965 and the invaluable introduction written by James Laver for a book entitled 'Ties' published by Seeley Service in 1968.

COLOR CIRCLES *page 52*

The Prismatic Circle, from a second edition of Moses Harris's book, in the library of The Royal Academy of Arts.
Photography John Freeman.
selected reading The Natural System of Colours by Moses Harris, originally published 1766. Theory of Colours – Johann Wolfgang von Goethe 1840 and books by Johannes Itten and Faber Birren.

CRACKERS *page 66*

Box of crackers and catalogue both from the collection of Tom Smith Co. Ltd. *Photography* Marianne Ford. Special thanks to the Tom Smith cracker factory who provided the necessary historical background and sound advice on the project. A Tom Smith cracker can be found in the Museum of Childhood in Edinburgh.

EASTER EGGS *page 88*

The Coronation Egg and coach are now in the Forbes Magazine Collection in New York. The photograph, which is reproduced with their permission, was kindly lent to us by Wartski.
selected reading Peter Carl Fabergé – Henry Charles Bainbridge 1949. Carl Fabergé: Goldsmith to the Imperial Court of Russia – Kenneth Snowman 1979. Fabergé: Imperial Eggs and other fantasies – Hermione Waterfield & Christopher Forbes 1978. Special thanks to Hermione Waterfield who provided the necessary introductions.

FLORA DELANICA *page 84*

The portrait of Mrs Delany is reproduced with kind permission of the National Portrait Gallery who supplied the photograph. Mrs Delany's 'paper mosaiks' are kept safely in the prints and drawings department of the British Museum.
Photography Marianne Ford.
selected reading Aspasia – C.E.Vulliamy 1935.
The autobiography and correspondence – Lady Llanover 1861.
Mrs Delany: Her Life and Times – Ruth Hayden 1980.

FOLDING FANS *page 86*

The Mask Fan from the Oldham Collection is in the Museum of Fine Arts, Boston, who kindly supplied the photograph. Special thanks to Susan Mayor of Christie's who suggested the museum where I might find a mask fan.
selected reading Pleasures of the Past – Iris Brooke 1955.
History of the Fan – George Wooliscroft Rhead 1910.
A Collector's Guide to Fans over the Ages – Bertha de Vere Green 1975.

GINGERBREAD *page 12*

Facsimile of a gingerbread cavalier taken from a mould in the collection of the Blaise Castle Museum, Hanbury, Bristol, to whom we have presented the facsimile. *Photography* John Freeman. Special thanks to Carvers & Gilders of Wandsworth who coloured, polished and gilded the cavalier. Alphabet mould from the Pinto collection of Treen in the Birmingham City Museum and Art Gallery who kindly supplied the photograph.
selected reading Food in England – Dorothy Hartley 1954.
Treen & other wooden bygones – E.H. Pinto 1969.
Special thanks to Christa Cercle who did invaluable research on the history of Gingerbread in Germany.

HOOKED RUGS *page 24*

Both English hooked rugs can be seen in period settings at the Museum of Lakeland Life and Industry in Kendal, who kindly took the photographs on our behalf. The American rug is from the American Museum at Claverton Manor, Bath, who supplied the photograph.
selected reading Rare hooked rugs – William Winthrop Kent 1941. Collecting Hooked Rugs – Elizabeth Jenkins Waugh 1927 and the chapter on 'Hooked Rugs' by Virginia Parslow in the Concise Encyclopaedia of American Antiques 1958.

KAI-AWASE *page 70*

Utamaro's illustration is in the collection of prints and drawings at the British Museum. *Photography* British Museum. The Shell game is from the collection of Kosu Kobunka Kaikan, Kyoto, Japan. It is reproduced by courtesy of the Japan Foundation. Special thanks to the Japanese Embassy, Mr Victor Harris at the British Museum and Mr William Tilley of Christie's, without whom there would have been no historical page!
selected reading (with a Japanese translator at hand) Japanese Games and their equipment – Nihon no Bijutsu 1968. Kai-awase – Tatsuji Okuma 1974.

KITES *page 74*

The kite with the portrait of Tametomo comes from the collection of Tal Streeter who kindly permitted us to reproduce it. Kunisada's kite fliers is in the collection of oriental prints at the Victoria & Albert Museum. The photograph is from the Hamlyn Group Picture Library. Special thanks to Ambrose and Nicolette Lloyd who suggested the illustration.
selected reading Art of the Japanese Kite – Tal Streeter 1974. Toys of Other Days – Mrs Neville Jackson 1908. Kites and Kite Flying – Ambrose Lloyd & Nicolette Thomas 1978.

KNITTING *page 20*

A detail from the painting, The Madonna of Bexterhude, from Kunstalle, Hamburg. *Photography* Ralph Kleinkempel. The Wensley Dale Knitters, an illustration from a book in the library of the Victoria and Albert Museum. *Photography* John Freeman.
selected reading Stockings for a Queen – M & A Grass 1967. History of Knitting – Heinz Edgar Kiewe 1976. The Rural Life of England – William Howitt 1838.

KNUCKLEBONES *page 26*

The Astragalus Players from the National Museum of Naples. *Photography* Vincenzo Carcavallo. Special thanks to Paola Fletcher of Trovarobe Limited, London, who located and arranged for us to borrow the photograph. A set of Knucklebones from the collection of the National Toy Museum in Rottingdean. *Photography* Marianne Ford, with kind permission of the Royal Pavilion Art Gallery and Museums, Brighton.

LACQUER *page 78*

Both examples come from the Victoria and Albert Museum. *Photography* V & A Crown Copyright.
selected reading Oriental Lacquer – Kurt Herberts 1959. Japanese Lacquer Ware – Tomio Yoshino 1959. A History of Japanese Lacquerwork – B. von Rague 1976.

LINO-CUTS *page 22*

'Broadlands' is reproduced with kind permission of Michael Parkin Fine Art Limited, who specialise in lino-cut prints and kindly lent us the photograph.
selected reading The Art & Craft of Lino Cutting & Printing – Claude Flight 1957. Lino-Cuts – Claude Flight 1927, and a booklet The Infancy and Development of Linoleum Floorcloth by its inventor Frederick Walton 1957.

MAKE-UP *page 72*

Grimshaw's watercolour of Grimaldi from the Museum of London, who supplied the photograph.
selected reading History of Make-Up – Maggie Angeloglou 1970. Fashions in Make-Up – Richard Corson 1972. Powder & Paint – Neville Williams 1957.

MARBLED PAPERS *page 8*

A detail from a Deccani Marbled Picture in the National Museum, Janpath, New Delhi. *Photography* Tejbir Singh. Special thanks to Mr and Mrs Hans Schmoller who commissioned the photograph and kindly suggested we should use it. Marbled papers on the cover are from the Hirsch collection at the British Museum. *Photography* British Museum.
selected reading The Art of Marbling – C.W. Woolnagh 1853. The Art of Bookbinding – J.W. Zaehnsdorf 1880. A History of English Craft Bookbinding Technique – B. Middleton 1963.

MINIATURE SHOPS *page 82*

One of a number of butcher's shops on display at the Bethnal Green Museum. *Photography* V & A Crown Copyright. Incidentally, those found in the tomb of Meket Re are in the collection of the Metropolitan Museum of Art in New York.
selected reading A History of Dolls Houses – Flora Gill Jacobs 1953. The Encyclopaedia of Toys – Constance Eileen King 1978. Children's Toys throughout the Ages – Leslie Daiken 1953.
Special thanks to Marie-Anne von Simson who translated a section of Das Puppenhaus, a specialist book on the subject by L. von Wilckens 1978 and to Camilla Brown who bought it on my behalf.

MONEY BOXES *page 14*

The Chute Hoard Money Box from the Museum of Devizes. *Photography* Wiltshire Archaeological and Natural History Society. Uncle Sam, the mechanical money box which can be seen in a number of toy collections in America, is reproduced with kind permission of the National Gallery of Washington. Incidentally the pottery money box from the Min Dynasty is in the Metropolitan Museum in New York.
selected reading Treasury of American Design – Clarence Hornung 1950. Cavalcade of Toys (N.Y.) – R & L Freeman 1942. Penny Banks – Carole Rogers 1977 and the booklet Money Boxes by Leonard W. Durham.

MOSAICS *page 18*

Salome from St. Mark's Cathedral, Venice. *Photography* Scala, Milan. Special thanks to Paola Fletcher of Trovarobe Limited, London, who located the photograph and arranged for us to borrow it. Medusa from the Roman Villa at Bignor, Sussex, who kindly supplied both this photograph and the geometric mosaic on the cover.
selected reading Mosaics – Ferdinando Rossi 1968. Life in Roman Britain – Anthony Birley 1964, and the invaluable entry in The Oxford Companion to Art.

PAINTED FINISHES *page 62*

The illustrations come from the Van der Burg's book which is in the library of the Victoria and Albert Museum. *Photography* John Freeman.
selected reading School of Painting for the Imitation of Woods and Marbles – A.R. and P. Van der Burg 1878. The Decorative Painters and Glaziers Guide – Nathaniel Whittock 1827. Marbling and Graining – John Parry 1949.

PAPER *page 58*

Hokusai's wood block print from the Arthur B. Duel Collection at the Fogg Art Museum, Harvard University, who kindly supplied the photograph.
selected reading Papermaking through Eighteen Centuries – Dard Hunter 1930. Papermaking – Dard Hunter 1943. A Brief History of Papermaking – R.L. Hills 1979. The North Western Museum of Science and Industry which includes the National Paper Museum who occasionally give demonstrations of Papermaking, and print a comprehensive leaflet on the subject.

PAPIER MÂCHÉ *page 16*

The Siamese Mask from the Riebeck Collection is in the Museum fur Volkerkunde, Berlin. *Photography* Bildarchiv Preussischer Kulturbesitz. Special thanks to Professor and Mrs von Simson who obtained the museum's permission and suggested the photographers.
selected reading Masks of the World – John Gregor 1936. English Papier Maché of the Georgian and Victorian Periods – Shirley Spaulding DeVoe 1971. Papier Maché in Great Britain and America – Jane Toller 1962.

PATCHWORK *page 64*

T.W. Wood's painting belongs to the Royal College of Surgeons of England who kindly permitted us to reproduce it. The facsimile of a Victorian patchwork cushion is in the collection of the interior designer Michael Carleton, who kindly allowed me to photograph it. The quilt, from which only a detail is shown, is from the extensive collection of American Folk Art at the Shelburne Museum in Vermont, who supplied the photograph.
selected reading Patchwork – Averil Colby 1958.
The Development of Embroidery in America – Candice Wheeler 1921. America's Quilts and Coverlets – C.L. Stafford & R. Bishop 1974.

POMANDERS *page 10*

Flemish Pomander, a rare example, acquired by 'La Vieille Russie' in New York who kindly lent us the photograph. While jewelled pomanders are located in the jewellery section of a museum – earlier and more practical examples can often be found among displays of herbal remedies and early medicine such as those in the Museum of London and on display in the Wellcome Gallery at the Science Museum.
selected reading History of Perfume – Frances Kennett 1975. Fragrance – Beverly Plummer 1975 and articles by R.H. Soden-Smith.

PORTABLE GARDENS *page 28*

The fern case from the People's Palace collections is on permanent display at their Museum of Local History in Glasgow. The photograph was kindly supplied by Glasgow Museums and Art Galleries. Dr. Beaumont at the quayside, a black and white illustration photographed from a magazine in the collection of The Royal Horticultural Society's Lindley Library. We coloured the photograph.
selected reading The Victorian Fern Craze – David Elliston Allen 1969. Rustic Adornments for Houses of Taste – Shirley Hibberd 1856. Decorative Cast Ironwork in Great Britain – Raymond Lister 1960.

QUILLS *page 60*

Van Scorel's painting from the Museum Boymans-van Beuningen, Rotterdam. *Photography* Dienst Germeetelijke Musea.
selected reading Writing Implements & Accessories – Joyce Whalley 1975 and a booklet Writing Materials of the East – Albertine Gaur 1979 published by the British Library.

QUILTING *page 44*

The Fairground Quilt is from the vast collection at the National Museum of History and Technology in Washington.
Photography The Smithsonian Institution. Fannie Lou Spelche's painting is reproduced by kind permission of E.P. Dutton, New York.
selected reading Artists in Aprons – C. Dewhurst & B. & M. MacDowell, USA 1979. The Pierced Quilt, an American Tradition – Jonathan Holstein 1975. Historical Costumes of England 1066–1968 – Nancy Bradfield 1938.

RATTLES *page 80*

The terracotta pig and bronze sistrum are from the British Museum. *Photography* The British Museum. The rattles from Ireland, Panama and Haida are from the Horniman Museum. *Photography* Marianne Ford. A special kiss to my niece Lily who permitted me to photograph her rattle.
selected reading A History of Toys – Antonia Fraser 1966. Infantilia – Arnold Haskall & Min Lewis 1971. Musical Instruments of the World – Diagram Group 1976.

REMEMBRANCE POPPIES *page 46*

Miss Oliver's pastel from the Imperial War Museum. *Photography* Marianne Ford. The Commemorative Stamp was kindly lent by Stanley Gibbons. Special thanks to the Colonel John MacRae Birthplace Society in Guelph Ontario who suggested we should use this illustration. They have a small museum in Guelph. Lutyens' sketch for the Cenotaph from the Courtauld Institute. *Photography* Geremy Butler. The poppy wreath from the Poppy Factory. *Photography* Marianne Ford.
selected reading Red for Remembrance – Anthony Brown 1971. Flowers of the world – Frances Perry 1962 and the leaflet 'The Poppy Emblem – How it all began' published by The Royal British Legion Press.

SHELLS IN DECORATION *page 38*

The Shell Grotto was photographed by Jeremy Whitaker.
selected reading Follies & Grottoes – Barbara Jones (revised 1974). The Georgians at Home – Elizabeth Burton 1967. Shell collecting – Peter S. Dance 1966.

SILHOUETTES *page 34*

The self portrait of Edouart was photographed direct from Mrs. Nevill Jackson's book 'Ancestors in Silhouette' published in 1920 by The Bodley Head, who kindly permitted us to reproduce my photograph. We were unable to trace the original. The child on a rocking horse, cut by Princess Elizabeth, daughter of George III, is reproduced by gracious permission of Her Majesty The Queen, from the collection in the Library at Windsor Castle. *Photography* A.C. Cooper.
selected reading History of Silhouettes – Mrs Nevill Jackson 1911. British Silhouettes – John Woodiwiss 1965. Profile Art through the Ages – R.L. Megroz 1948.

SLIDE WHISTLES *page 50*

The catalogue and its relevant page belong to the firm Barnes & Mullins. The piccolo swanee whistle is from the Horniman Museum. *Photography* Marianne Ford. I am particularly grateful to the present Mr. Barnes who was able to enlighten me on the subject and who gave me a present day Barnes & Mullins whistle to compare to ours. Special thanks to Carole Switzer who, while studying to be a librarian, did a literature search on the swanee whistle which she kindly sent me. This confirms that there is very little material available on the subject and only by gathering snippets from a wide range of books have I been able to include this project.

SOLITAIRE *page 48*

The watercolour of a young woman playing Solitaire is an illustration from a book in the library of the Victoria and Albert Museum. *Photography* John Freeman.
selected reading Board and Table games – R.C. Bell 1969. A History of Board Games other than Chess – H.J. Murray 1952.

STENCILING *page 68*

Both the stencil and the stencilled Buddha are in the Stein collection at the British Museum. The photographs are reproduced with kind permission of Kodansha. Special thanks to Dr Roderick Whitfield who suggested the illustrations which appear in his book 'Art of Central Asia: Paintings from Dunhuang' a magnificent work published in limited edition by Kodansha in collaboration with the British Museum.
selected reading Serindia (vol. II) – Sir Marc Aurel Stein 1921.
Early American Stencils – Janet Waring 1937.
The Book of Wallpaper – E.A. Entwistle 1954.
and an article written by Francis W. Reader for
The Archaeological Journal in 1938.

STRAW MARQUETRY *page 40*

All the straw marquetry came from the special collection of Norman Cross work in the Peterborough City Museum, who kindly allowed me to photograph it. The box on the cover is in the Luton Museum, who lent us the photograph.
selected reading Scrimshaw and Scrimshanders – E. Norman Flyderman 1972. Prisoners of War work 1756–1815 – Jane Toller 1965. Decorative straw work – Lettice Sandford & Philla Davis 1964.

THAUMATROPES *page 76*

Dr Paris's book with Cruikshank the Elder's illustration is in the British Library. *Photography* The British Museum.
The thaumatrope is in the collection of the Science Museum who supplied the photograph. The box comes from the Barnes Museum of Cinematography who kindly photographed it on our behalf.
selected reading Philosophy in Sport made Science in Earnest – John Ayrton Paris 1827.
Movement in Two Dimensions – Olive Cook 1963.

VALENTINES *page 42*

The Valentine is one of a collection presented to the Gunnersbury Park Museum in the London Borough of Ealing.
Photography Marianne Ford.
selected reading A History of Valentines – Ruth Webb Lee 1953. The Valentine and its origins – Frank Staff 1969, and a booklet produced by the Castle Museum in York entitled Valentines by Violet A. Wlock.

WHIRLIGIGS *page 32*

The witch on a broomstick is from the collection of Leo and Dorothy Rabkin promised to the Museum of American Folk Art in New York. *Photography* Helga Photo Studio.
selected reading American Folk Sculpture – Robert Bishop 1974. English Weathervanes – A.A. Needham 1953.
Toys of other days – Mrs Neville Jackson 1908.

WOODEN JOINTED DOLLS *page 56*

The Roman doll from the Museo Capitolino, Rome.
Picture source Weidenfeld and Nicolson Archives. Florence Upton's illustration was taken from the book in the British Library. *Photography* The British Library.
selected reading Children's Toys of Bygone Days – Karl Grober 1928 Dolls and Doll Makers – Mary Hillier 1968.
Treen and other wooden bygones – E.H. Pinto 1969.

Generally – **compulsory reading**

Consulted on almost every subject; the Oxford English Dictionary, the Dictionary of National Biography and the Penguin Dictionary of Decorative Arts by John Fleming and Hugh Honour.